PULPWOOD DAYS
Volume 1: Editors You Want To Know

EDITED BY

John Locke

Off-Trail Publications

Elkhorn, California

PULPWOOD DAYS
Volume 1: Editors You Want To Know

Copyright © 2007 Off-Trail Publications

ISBN-10: 0-9786836-2-5
ISBN-13: 978-0-9786836-2-7

All Rights Reserved. No part of this book may be reproduced or transmitted in any form by any means, electronic or mechanical, including photocopying, recording or by an information storage and retrieval system, without written permission of the publisher, except where permitted by law.

OFF-TRAIL PUBLICATIONS
2036 Elkhorn Road
Castroville, CA 95012
offtrail@redshift.com

Printed in the United States of America
First Printing: March 2007

FRONT COVER FAN:
Fantastic Adventures, **August 1943**
Robert Gibson Jones (cover artist), Ray Palmer (editor)
Brief Stories, **September 1929**
Elliott Dold (art), W. Adolphe Roberts (ed)
Oriental Stories, **Spring 1932**
Margaret Brundage (art), Farnsworth Wright (ed)
Triple-X Magazine, **March 1930**
George Rozen (art), Roscoe Fawcett (ed)
War Aces, **June 1932**
William Reusswig (art), Carson Mowre (ed)
Love Story Magazine, **July 26, 1930**
Modest Stein (art), Daisy Bacon (ed)
Railroad Stories, **October 1932**
Emmett Watson (art), Freeman H. Hubbard (ed)
Far West Illustrated, **July 1927**
Charles Russell (art), Frank E. Blackwell (ed)

CONTENTS

Introduction *by John Locke* 7

EDITORS ARE GOOD SCOUTS *by Thomas Thursday*........ 9
   The Author & Journalist, July 1925

MEETING THE EDITORS IN PERSON *by Albert W. Stone*
   The Author & Journalist
   INTRODUCTION 15
      August 1926
   FRANK E. BLACKWELL & ALICE STROPE 21
      September 1926
   HARRY MAULE, A.H. BITTNER, ANTHONY RUD 27
      October 1926
   M. WHITE, JR., R. SIMPSON, R.A. MARTINSEN 33
      November 1926
   ADVENTURE, EVERYBODY'S, ARTHUR E. SCOTT,
      HAROLD HERSEY 41
      December 1926
   GENERAL IMPRESSIONS 48
      January 1927

DAMNING THE EDITOR *by Arthur E. Scott*............... 54
   The Author & Journalist, January 1928

THE ENTERPRISING AUTHOR *by Emil Zubryn* 57
   Writer's Digest, March 1928

AN EXPERIMENT IN COOPERATION *by Harold Hersey* ... 60
   The Author & Journalist, November 1928

A LETTER FROM ARTHUR J. BURKS 63
   Writers' Markets and Methods, June 1929

EDITORS YOU WANT TO KNOW
   The Author & Journalist
   W. ADOLPHE ROBERTS *by Frances Dublin* 67
      July 1929

EDITORS YOU WANT TO KNOW (cont.)
    CAPTAIN W.H. FAWCETT *by W.E. Hawkins* 69
        August 1929
    HARRY E. MAULE *by William MacLeod Raine* 73
        August 1929
    DAISY BACON *by Joa Humphrey*.................... 77
        September 1929
    EDWIN BAIRD *by MacKinley Kantor*................ 79
        November 1929
    LAWRENCE LEE.................................... 83
        January 1930
    HARRIET A. BRADFIELD *by B.Virginia Lee*........... 85
        August 1930
    A.H. BITTNER *by B.Virginia Lee*..................... 87
        August 1930
    FARNSWORTH WRIGHT *by E. Hoffmann Price* 89
        October 1930

SHOOTING AT THE MOON *by Wallace R. Bamber* 92
    The Author & Journalist, November 1930

WHAT IN THUNDER *IS* THEIR POLICY?
    by Richard A. Martinsen 99
    The Author & Journalist, January 1931

WHAT AN EDITOR REALLY THINKS *by Carson Mowre*....110
    Writer's 1931 Year Book

TRAINED SEALS *by Freeman H. Hubbard*.................117
    The Author & Journalist, October 1931

ON RELATIONS WITH EDITORS *by Ray Palmer* 121
    The Author & Journalist, April 1942

MISSION TO MANHATTAN *by H. Wolff Salz*.............. 124
    Writer's Digest, March 1944

A YANK AT YALE *by Mort Weisinger* 130
    Writer's Digest, September 1944

HITCH IT TO A HORSE *by Robert A.W. Lowndes* 139
    Writer's 1949 Year Book

THE GOOD LIFE 154
    Writer's Digest, November 1950

WILD EDITORS I HAVE KNOWN *by Thomas Thursday*.... 158
    Author & Journalist, August 1952

Index   163

Introduction

THIS COLLECTION, FROM WRITERS' MAGAZINES published during the Pulp Era, focuses on the editors, the tireless and often anonymous people who selected the stories, whipped them into shape, advised and often befriended the writers, and got the pulps out on time. More times than not, anyway.

The first point to make is a slight warning. Many obscure figures receive a lot of attention here, while many of the greats receive very little—if they're to be found at all. This is not a comprehensive study of the most famous or important people. The articles chosen were those that best described the working life and experience of pulp magazine editors, and there simply weren't many candidates fitting within that vague yet narrow definition. Many editors chose not to share their lives with the industry press. Who knows why? Too busy, not interested, didn't need more freelance submissions, didn't need the money. Some editor-written articles consisted exclusively of counsel to writers—storytelling craft—and these were not chosen, although that kind of advice spills over into the included material. The good news is that the obscure figures had as much to say as the famous, and their careers, described in notes preceding the articles, often illuminate forgotten corners in pulp magazine history.

We reprint two series. *Meeting the Editors in Person* is included in its entirety. *Editors You Want To Know*, from which we filched our subtitle, roped in a variety of magazine editors; all the pulp personalities are included here.

One thing that became apparent in assembling this collection is that pulp editors were a varied breed. Some, like Ray Palmer or Freeman H. Hubbard, were lifers at heart and, once in the game, spent the majority of their careers as editors; like many other editors, they also wrote when they found the time. On the opposite end of the spectrum were people who passed through the pulps until their luck ran out—Dick Martinsen or Wally Bamber—and went on, we assume, to other careers in other places. When the abundant opportunities of the Roaring Twenties gave way to the Depression, many industry professionals must have found it hard to stay employed. Many pulp editors came from newspaper work, and it's likely that's where many of them went after disappearing from the pulps. Some editors, like W. Adolphe Roberts and Lawrence Lee, are here simply because they were swept up in one of the series. They happened to be holding editorial positions when the two series were composed. Both men distinguished themselves in post-pulp careers. Lee, one suspects, came to the New York publishing world to sow his wild literary oats before finding his true calling; while Roberts was simply paying the bills until his writing became self-sustaining. Irma Kalish is another person who did service to the pulps in the early years of her professional life. She might have stayed and become a big name, except that entering the pulps in the late '40s proved bad timing. It was excellent timing for television, however, where she, and her writer-husband, made their marks instead. Another lifer, "Doc" Lowndes, pooh-poohed the idea that the pulps were dying in a pair of 1952 articles, then did his best to keep them alive through the end of the decade.

These are a few of the fascinating people to be found in these pages, rediscovered, many of them, for the first time since they passed from the pulp scene so many years ago.

And for all those, famous or otherwise, who didn't make the cut, this book is certainly not the last word on pulp editors. Other articles which fit more naturally into other thematic categories, we hope to include in future volumes in this series.

— John Locke
February 2007

[*The Author & Journalist*, July 1925]

Editors Are Good Scouts
Thomas Thursday

[No consideration of pulp editors would be complete without the contributions of Tom Thursday (1894-19??), one of the least-known but longest-enduring fictioneers. He talks about acceptance and rejection with good cheer here, in the heady days of the Jazz Age when selling stories was a lark. When the bottom dropped out a few years later, Thursday's editors turned into "idiotors."]

SINCE ABANDONING MYSELF to the spare-time use of the insidious typewriter I have sold for cash—not glory—about 154 short stories and 21 articles. The yarns were supposed to be humorous. However, with the possible exception of Dr. Ellis Parker Butler and Sherwood Anderson, I'm probably the worst writer of humor either on or off the earth. Some day I hope to be one-tenth as proficient as H.C. Witwer, by all odds the most prolific and accomplished designer of really funny yarns that these States ever have produced. (Highbrows—be good!) All this by way of an opening—a guy has got to get started somehow, huh?

During the few years I have meddled in the hectic game of get-by-the-editor, I have been treated with a consideration and courtesy that I have not deserved. Show me the man or woman who claims that beginning writers have no chance with the current crop of editors and I'll show you a cross between a Greenwich Village bum and a literary flop! Gosh, with the deluge of magazines on the stands today it seems to me that anyone, even with the least spark of talent, should be able to peddle his or her wares to *some* market. Of course if you're a stickler for what they call high literary art—whatever that is—all right, that's your affair. Starve in your garret, if you wish, and perhaps posterity will erect a tin statue to you after you have ascended to heaven. As for me, well, posterity be blowed—here comes the landlord! In short, what the hell do I care for posterity? Imagine the egoism of the writer who boasts that he's writing for posterity! Also, take a peek at the shape of his head.

For our text today I'm going to broadcast some letters from a number of famous editors—letters written to me in reference to my various contributions to the—er—classic literature of America. (Quit yer laughing, Shakespeare!)

I sold the first story I wrote to Henry Wilton Thomas, former editor of *Top-Notch Magazine*. At the time I knew nothing of magazines or magazine "slants." More, I had never read a copy of *Top-Notch*. The reason I submitted the yarn to that periodical was that I happened to find an old issue in the subway. I got the address, and away went the gem. Bing—just like that! As I say, I knew nothing of the magazine or the writing profession, or, as the college professors call it, the writing game. From the tip of my nose to the tip of my toes, I'm a circus showman, and one-night stands give one little or no time to go in for art and literature. I'm still a showman—not knowing any better, I guess. I speak along these lines merely to show you what little equipment I started out with to battle the demon editors. (Woof—when I think of my magnificent innocence at that time I could actually weep!)

A week later I received this letter:

Dear Mr. Thursday:
"A Stroke of Genius" goes. Check this week for thirty-five cents, or will you have it in postage stamps?

Sincerely,
H.W. Thomas, Editor.

I was inclined to think that somebody was kidding me. On the other hand, I was innocent enough to believe that perhaps thirty-five cents was their regular rate of payment for a 2500-word story. I replied that I'd be tickled silly to accept the thirty-five cents—in cash. By return mail I received a check for forty dollars. Ain't editors crool? After that I got busy and sold the kindly and ever-patient Thomas several thousand dollars' worth of gems. I wish space would permit me to show you, who still think that editors are in league against your every effort, the many painstaking and instructive letters this humble scribe has received from H.W. Thomas, God bless 'im! Frankly, had I been in his place and he in mine, I would have taken a vicious delight in jamming four dollars' worth of rejection slips in each story that popped in.

Next on the air tonight, boys and girls, will be no less than "Always sincerely, R.H. Davis." Or, in round numbers, Robert Hobart Davis, of the Frank A. Munsey Company. Davis has discovered about every writer but Moses. More, he's a darn good guy to have in your corner. Get him interested in you and he will stick by you until the checks come home. But if he drops you it's a ten-to-one shot that you're a palooka, as they remark in the fight game. Another thing, he'll give you straight-from-the-shoulder advice—he doesn't stall with a writer. I have in my files about fifty letters from R.H.D. I will start off by displaying the rejective ones—I have more of the other kind, but his toss-backs are more interesting.

Once I sent him a boxing story, entitled "Ringing the Dumbbell." It flew back, attached to this:

My dear Thursday:
You didn't ring in this time. I apologize to you.

Always sincerely, R.H. Davis.

Here's another one he didn't like:

Dear T.T.:
 By gosh, you've got a new one on the old mortgage. Nix on the old stuff. Young love survives all time. And listen, cul, make it plausible. Don't try to jam something down their throats they won't swallow.
 Happy New Year nevertheless!

Always sincerely,
R.H. Davis.

Here's another kick in the sit-spot:

Dear Thursday:
 Cut out them one-night stands and take a weekend on the quiet. You need a rest. This manuscript is a piece of Cheddar.

Yours as ever,
R.H. Davis.

And listen to this:

My Dear Thursday:
 This is a complete, absolute flop. I think these domestic stories would he a damned sight better if you kept your family at home. Blooey for this!

Ever sincerely,
R.H. Davis.

How can you get mad at a guy like Davis? Note that there is no hemming or hawing. He doesn't like a story, and he says so. I'll say he does! The fact that these rejected-by-Davis stories all sold later to other editors doesn't mean a thing, except this: They liked 'em, and Davis didn't. What's more, I was *paid* for 'em and, just between you and me, that's that.

Here's another dose from Old Doc Davis:

My dear T.T.:
 In the name of God and the Twelve Apostles, Mr. Man, give me something that I can believe.
 It almost dislocates my arm to sign a letter criticizing you. You are throttling a great gift for humor by taxing it to such improbabilities.

Always sincerely,
R.H. Davis.

I sent him a yarn, entitled "The False Alarm Murder." Tune in on this comeback:

Dear Thursday:
There's more than one false-alarm in this story.

Ever yours,
Davis.

Before I take Mons. Davis off the air, I'd like to broadcast a few of his "acceptance" radios. Short and sweet:

Dear T.T.:
I enclose a check.

Ever sincerely,
R.H. Davis.

No editor need write more to me! And this:

My dear T.T.:
You rapped 'em that time. Take another belt at the family. Here's a check. *Gracias.*

Always sincerely,
R.H. Davis.

More music:

Dear T.T.:
You hit 'em hard with "Art For Artie." I got forty laughs. Shoot a check through next week.

Ever yours,
Davis.

So much for Robert H. Davis, probably the best known editor in these States. Frankly, I like to play with him. He lacks that false dignity that seems to embalm a few editors I might mention, but won't. He calls a spade a spade—and a fathead a fathead. Atta boy, Bob!

Of course, in reference to these rejected stories, I might have answered Davis and argued the point. That would have been foolish. Never, *never*, boys and girls, argue with an editor. Shoot him, drown him, sock him on the chin, or even hang him; but for the love of Pegasus, don't argue with him. You haven't got a chance!

Next on our program is Mr. Arthur E. Scott, able successor to Mr. Henry W. Thomas, as editor of *Top-Notch Magazine*, one of the most successful of the Street & Smith group. Another good scout! If he thinks a story has a chance of being good *Top-Notch* material, he'll go so far as to help you rewrite it. Fair enough, what? For example, just a short time ago, I submitted a gem to him and it came back with this letter:

Dear Mr. Thursday:
"It's Great to Be Great" isn't long enough to the theme. However, not much more is required. Suppose a week or a couple of weeks pass before Wickpick shows up, looking for a job. He gets thrown out—as you have it—and then you want to have him act as spokesman for the freaks, who quit, and get hired on the strength of getting the freaks back, who are all outside, a little way off, tired and hungry but afraid to approach the boss for reinstatement....
Don't you see that this gets the story somewhere? As you have it, it all ends in a fizzle.

Sincerely yours,
Arthur E. Scott,
Editor.

This bit of kind advice improved the story fifty percent. I followed Scott's specific instructions, submitted the revised copy, and promptly received a fat check. And the point is this: Scott was willing to take his valuable editorial time to show me what was wrong. It doesn't matter a tinker's tink whether I agreed with his version or not. He wanted it that way and he got it. And why shouldn't he have what he wants? He's *paying* for it, isn't he? Sure—and he's right. I'll be darned if I'll buy anything that doesn't exactly suit me—even socks!

Next I'll try and entertain you with a few letters from the heavy editors. I have tried the big-time magazines only a few times, believing that I'm not quite ripe for their markets. But I found them very courteous, to say the least.

This is Mr. Loren Palmer talking, from station *Collier's,* in reference to one of my yarns:

My dear Mr. Thursday:
This is not the kind of story we would buy for *Collier's*, because we prefer humor to farce.
It is very amusing reading, however, and written by a story-writer. When you have something of a different type to submit, I shall be glad to read it.

Sincerely yours,
Loren Palmer.

So I hadda sell that gem to one of the print-paper magazines, and may the saints protect 'em! But it shows that the big boys give you rumble, doesn't it?

And now we have Mr. William C. Lengel, at the time managing editor of *Hearst's International,* and now representing the Hearst interests in England.

Not knowing Lengel from Mr. Adam, I addressed him as "Dear Bill." Here's the comeback:

> Dear Tom:
> If you don't look out you're going to land here! "Good Morning, Mr. Jones!" comes very near to being a winner. I'll promise you a very careful reading of anything you have.
>
> Sincerely yours,
> Wm. C. Lengel.

I next sent the story to *Short Stories* and—bing!—Harry Maule thought it good enough to pay for. Speaking of Maule, rest assured that he's another good scout. When he rejects, it sounds like this:

> Dear Mr. Thursday:
> Sorry, but I'm afraid that "Robinson Crew So" is a bit too farfetched to get by with our literal-minded public, so I've got to let it go back to you herewith. If you won't lose patience with us, we won't lose patience with you. Here's hoping,
>
> Yours sincerely,
> H.E. Maule.

Pretty decent letter, that. Any writer who'd get peeved at Maule for that sort of rejection is a grade-A boob—and a boob is a terrific thing, believe me, Barnum! As to that particular story, it was sent to our old friend R.H. Davis, and—what do you know?—it was the means of starting a series with him that has been running for two years and is still going. But that doesn't mean that Maule is a flop as an editor. Not at all. It simply wasn't his sort of yarn, see? But it *was* the sort of bait that Davis was after. That editors have different policies, Allah—and all the other gods—be praised!

Well, thanks for listening—I'm signing off now. I may be on the air again sometime—if Hawkins will let me. Meantime, good hunting to you all!

[*The Author & Journalist*, August 1926]

Meeting the Editors in Person
Albert William Stone

[This six-part series is worth less as journalism than its length implies. Stone pads the narrative with quaint and irrelevant details, e.g. "A quietly dressed young woman is Miss Strope, with the pink glow of perfect health in her cheeks . . ." Still, Stone's travels from office to office convey a fictioneer's sense of being in the moment, which endows the series with no little charm. A highlight is Stone's attempt to visit all the pulp publishers on foot, not realizing how far apart they are. We experience the immensity of Manhattan through the eyes of a first-time visitor. (November) :: Of historical note, Stone divides the fiction magazine market into "all-fictions" vs. "higher class." He does, however, refer to the "all-fictions" a couple of times as "pulp" or "wood-pulp," some of the earliest known uses of these terms. "The pulps" would not be common nomenclature until the late '20s. :: Stone accurately sums up his writing career to date in the first part. His remained a steady seller through the end of the decade, appearing numerous times in *Ace-High, Short Stories, Far West, Western Trails*, etc. The early '30s show the diversification into mystery fiction hinted at in the November article: *Detective Story, Clues*. But his career seems to have petered out about that time, as well.]

I HAVE BEEN SELLING FICTION, more or less steadily, for more than eight years. In that time I have disposed of approximately three hundred short stories, to twenty-three magazines, twenty of them of the class known as "popular." Eighteen of these magazines are published in New York.

For the last two years I have been making my living at writing fiction. In other words, there are those who would credit me with having "arrived" (although I haven't, really), because I seem to have reached the stage where I can live and support my family upon what editors pay me for the stories I write. Virtually my entire income is represented in what the postman brings me.

Up to a month or so ago I had never seen a magazine editor—with two exceptions. As both of these gentlemen edit publications to which I have never sold anything, they don't count in this confession. What I mean to say is, I had never seen any of the editors who had been buying my work; and yet my sales have been mounting with satisfactory rapidity.

Occasionally I have met brother writers, usually fellows much farther up the ladder than I, who assured me that I ought to go to New York and meet the editors in person.

"You'll gain by it," they declared. "Personal contact; that's the thing. Meet 'em face to face. Nothing like personal meetings to cement friendships. It's true in all other lines of activity, isn't it? Well, then!"

Frankly, the advantages of meeting the editors in person had always been rather vague to me. Don't they invariably declare that "the story's the thing"? Of what avail is personal contact, then? An author can't sell a yarn to a hardboiled editor by virtue of his persuasive ability. The story must measure up to that editor's standard.

Nevertheless, I felt that it would be pleasant to meet some of the gentlemen anyway. I was curious, for one thing, to see what they looked like. There was Frank E. Blackwell, editor-in-chief of *Detective Story*, *Western Story* and *True Western Stories*. For years he had been writing me kindly letters and sending me checks. Miss Alice Strope, his efficient associate editor—what of her? She often bought, and she frequently rejected. Her letters were cordial and filled with wise counsel. And there was Mr. Kelly, of Fiction House, Inc., publishers of *Action Stories*, *The Lariat*, *Northwest Stories*, etc.; a gentleman who can say more in less space than any other editorial writer I have ever dealt with, by the way. To say nothing of Mr. Martinsen, the "authors' contact" man of the Fiction House staff; of Harry E. Maule, the chief mogul of the Doubleday-Page magazines, *Short Stories*, *The Frontier* and *West*; of A.H. Bittner, Ralph Perry, Anthony Rud and others on the Doubleday-Page staff; of Harold Hersey, of the Clayton publications, *Ace-High*, *Cowboy Stories*, etc.; of the never-to-be-forgotten "Bob" Davis, of the Munsey staff; of Matthew White, Jr., and Mr. Titherington, of *Argosy*, *All-Story* and *Munsey's*, respectively; of Robert Simpson, of the *Mystery Magazine*; and so on, ad infinitum.

Would it pay me to make the long journey to New York to meet these gentlemen? And, if so, how?

"Do it," other writers counseled me. "You won't regret it."

Well, I went. I remained long enough to have interviews with thirteen editors in the flesh. I did it all in five days with Sunday intervening. And at this writing, safely back in Denver and once more pegging away at the typewriter, I can honestly and sincerely declare that, in my case at least, meeting the editors has been a profitable, as well as a rarely pleasant, experience.

In the present article there will be space only to summarize some of the benefits received. These benefits are found in the answers to certain questions which writers are constantly propounding. Perhaps I had better set these questions down as I go along, answer them from my individual experience and illustrate my answers with recitals of things told me by editors during our interviews. Here they are:

Q: Can a writer learn more specifically what editors want in the way of stories, from personal contact?

A: Decidedly, yes. One editor spent an hour and a half outlining the kind of stories he desired, illustrating his talk with examples taken from experience.

When he had finished, I had definitely relegated to the scrapheap several fundamental errors I had been making for years. Incidentally, this editor has rejected only one yarn from my pen since, and that one he stated was simply not the kind he was using. He turned it over to another magazine for further consideration. At this writing I have not heard from the second editor.

Q. Should writers read and study the magazines they are aiming at before they prepare their stories?

A. Usually, they should. I found but one editor who advised otherwise. All the others stressed, with emphasis, the necessity for this precaution. One editor went so far as to declare that the average author would increase his sales to a point close to one hundred percent, by first studying the magazines aimed at. Another declared that more than half the failures on the part of authors to sell their work could be traced to this lack of "sales sense," as he expressed it.

Q. Do editors like personal letters with manuscripts submitted?

A. Some of them do, some of them don't. One editor assured me that he likes them, and would rather have a personal letter with a story than not. Another, on the other hand, declared with considerable warmth that he "never reads 'em." A third said that they do no harm provided they are short and have some point to them. A fourth asserted that such letters do no harm, but, conversely, neither do they do any good. My conclusion, therefore, is that some editors really like personal letters, provided they are not fulsome or obviously designed to aid in selling the story, and that others pay little or no attention to them. It seems to be up to the writer to exercise selectivity with reference to the particular editor with whom he may be dealing, and gauge his letter-writing activities accordingly.

Q. Do editors like to receive personal calls from authors?

A. I should say that they do, provided the author is one with whom they have been corresponding and of whom they have been buying some manuscript. Some so-called authors are pests, of course. They will waste valuable time if permitted to do so. Against this kind the editors have erected a protective shield. But the author who calls purely on business, states his business clearly and concisely and departs as soon as the business is finished, is always welcome. Editors recognize that a part of their duties is to meet writers in person. The out-of-town author who calls is sure of an audience, at least if the editor has been doing business with him or has evinced an interest in his work.

Q. Are editors willing to help authors with suggestions?

A. They are, invariably. In fact, they welcome the opportunity to do so. A writer who shows talent and adaptability is always considered a "find." I cannot stress this too strongly. A "find" is to an editor what a "strike" is to the sportsman on a fishing trip. He takes personal and professional pride in developing the new writer, and in exhibiting the writer's name in his table of contents. Of course, the writer must show something besides talent merely. He must be turning out work showing considerable promise, and especially the promise of eventually rounding it into the particular form and shape required by the magazine of which the editor in question is the editorial head.

Q. Is there really a wide demand for popular fiction among New York editors, or is the supply so great that the new writer is seriously handicapped in his efforts to break in?

A. I found that the competition between rival magazines in New York is incredibly keen. Some of the editors admit it frankly. The reason is obvious. Where a few years ago there were only one or two so-called "popular" magazines, today there are scores. One publishing house alone issues eleven different magazines, several of them coming out weekly and others twice a month. One company pays out for magazine material alone, about $100,000 a month. Another's annual expenditures in this connection approximate $750,000 a year. The competition between editors for material, therefore, was never so keen as now. They literally pounce upon a promising new author. This is not an exaggeration; it is a cold business fact, and is recognized as such in New York. However, the new writer must produce the goods to sell, even to this teeming market. He cannot dispose of shoddy. The rivalry between editors is based upon the necessity of finding material meeting the more or less exacting requirements of their readers. They will not buy anything that happens to be offered, simply because the authors declare it to be fiction. "Produce the goods," and you will be astonished and gratified to find that the sale of your work is merely a matter of intelligent submission.

Q. What is the condition of the so-called higher class fiction magazine market? Does it pay a writer to try for it?

A. I was informed by one editor who seemed to know that writing for the "highbrow" fiction magazines is a precarious undertaking for the average author. Even the well-known names, he asserted, would have a struggle if they depended upon that class of market alone. But most of them do not. Many of them write also for the all-fiction market under noms de plume; and in the majority of cases they make more income from the all-fiction market than from the higher class magazines. The latter give them valuable advertising, perhaps; but as the higher class magazine market is necessarily limited, as compared to that represented by the all-fiction magazines, many wise writers turn out reams of action fiction at lower rates, to augment their incomes. I was surprised to learn that some of the best known names appearing in the tables of contents of such all-fiction magazines as *Argosy All-Story, Western Story, Detective Story, Adventure, Short Stories, The Frontier,* etc., are really noms de plume of writers who may be found in *The Saturday Evening Post, Cosmopolitan, Red Book, Pictorial Review, Collier's,* etc. Thus, you see, the all-fiction market is not to be despised. It constitutes the financial backing of many a famous author.

Q. Is a literary agent of value to an author?

A. This depends upon the author, and upon the agent. There are good and bad agents. There are agents who will handle only the work of dependable, prolific, high-grade writers, and cannot be induced to deal with any other kind. There are agents, also, who will handle anything that is fiction, depending upon volume for their profit. There are discriminating agents, and there are non-discriminating agents. And, of course there are unscrupulous, dishonest agents, who merely prey upon inexperienced writers.

I learned in New York that certain agents have no standing whatever with editors, and that others stand so high that a mere statement from them that they have a good story, adaptable to the magazine in question, means a sale. On the whole, I should say that writers should market their own work until they discover one of the dependable agents.

Q. What rates may a writer look forward to getting, if he continues to progress in his profession, from the all-fiction market especially?

A. The new writer may reasonably expect one cent a word from the average all-fiction magazine, to start with. Some pay less, and a few pay more. An advance to a cent and a half may be sought and received after selling to such magazines for, say, a year—provided the sales have been of reasonable frequency. Two cents will be paid by most of the all-fictions at the end of two years or more; but at this point the limit has been reached in the majority of cases, I believe. Most editors with whom I talked spoke of two cents a word as their limit, although admitting that in exceptional cases they would pay more. A few of the editors pay up to three and a half cents, usually to older and more dependable writers, and a very few up to five cents.

Q. Is it dangerous to success to turn out work too rapidly?

A. I was surprised to find that the average all-fiction magazine editor cares nothing whatever for the speed with which a writer turns out work, provided it reaches the standard of quality he demands. Personally, I have written two short stories, of five thousand words each, in a single week, submitted them both in the same envelope to an editor, and received his check for the pair by return mail. This same editor assured me that if I could turn out three or four reasonably good short stories a week, he would buy them all without delay, and would be "mighty glad to get them." Some writers turn out fiction so rapidly, that it is necessary to run their stories under several different names, perhaps two or more in one issue. Editors often issue entire numbers of their magazines with only four or five contributors represented in the pages, although a dozen or more names may appear. Some authors are so prolific that, were their stories to appear with their real names over them all the time, readers would became satiated. In other words, there is a "saturation point" in the personal publicity accruing to writers through the use of their own names over their yarns, and the editors avoid reaching that point by the substitution of noms de plume.

It is doubtless true that too-rapid effort on the part of the average author means corresponding lowering of quality; but editors of the all-fiction magazines appear to pay little attention to this danger. What they are interested in is getting fiction of the class demanded by their readers and the policy of their magazines; they care nothing for the rapidity with which work is turned out and received.

Q. Is it a good plan to keep a manuscript in the mails until all possibility of sale is exhausted?

A. Yes, and no. Editors admitted to me that evidence of long travel, appearing in the form of old creases, finger marks, wrinkled paper, and so on, prejudices them in spite of themselves. One editor expressed astonishment when I told him I had sold him stories previously rejected by another editor. He indicated that he might not have purchased the stories had he known of this. However, many stories are purchased after repeated submissions; the safe plan is to rewrite the first and last pages of the manuscript each time it is returned, and other pages if they seem to require such treatment. After the seventh or eighth rejection, I should say, an entire revamping might be profitable; it usually is.

The foregoing is largely a series of impressions I received as a result of my interviews. In subsequent articles I shall go more into detail, repeating conversations I had with certain editors. The business advantage of such personal contacts is invaluable, I believe. In one instance I sold a series of stories at double the rate the magazine had previously been paying me; in another I was assured that if I would send a volume of salable material, I would receive better rates than I had been getting, with prospects of still better to come in the future. A few editors were kind enough to ask me to write something for them before I left New York. I was too busy, however, to do so.

Yes, it paid me, in dollars and cents, to go to New York. In one sale alone, of a story written since my return, I received forty-eight dollars more than I would have received had I not seen the editor in person; in fact, I probably would not have made the sale at all, since it was at his suggestion that I wrote the yarn along lines agreed upon between us. He knew what he wanted, and told me. I wrote what he wanted, and received a generous check for it.

In conclusion, I would say that if you have sold one or more editors at least five stories each, you can scarcely lose anything by going to New York and meeting the gentlemen—or ladies—in person.

[*The Author & Journalist*, September 1926]

Meeting the Editors in Person
Frank E. Blackwell and Alice Strope

[Notes on Blackwell accompany "The Enterprising Author." :: Alice Strope went on to edit *Crime Mysteries* at Dell.]

IT IS TRITE TO SAY that "editors are human." Of course they are. They wouldn't be editors if they were not. They are so human that they are ambitious, considerate, tolerant, broadminded, keen-visioned—and the reverse of these things when the weather is too hot or they have eaten too heartily of a heavy dinner. They are good tempered or bad, according to circumstances and their immediate reaction to them. They have their prejudices, for and against. They have their egotisms and their professional jealousies, expressed sometimes with subtlety and sometimes without. They've got what the man in the street would call "a hard job"; and since having conversed with a baker's dozen of them in New York, I take off my hat to them as gentlemen possessed of large quantities of brains, perception, judgment and the milk of human kindness.

The first one I saw, after arriving in New York, was Frank E. Blackwell of the Street & Smith Corporation.

Mr. Blackwell once replied to a letter of mine something as follows: "Don't get discouraged, old man. Writing is the most difficult field of endeavor. Keep right at it, and you'll win out."

So I was interested in meeting Mr. Blackwell. He is editor of three magazines—*Detective Story*, *Western Story* and *Far West Illustrated*. Miss Alice Strope is the associate editor of these three publications, two of them weeklies and the third a monthly. I had been selling them short stories over a period of more than five years. They had written me dozens of letters. Now I was to see them in person.

The Street & Smith building is several stories high, and crammed from basement to roof with visible and audible evidences of the great publishing business housed in it. You hear the linotype machines clatter and the presses rumble continuously. Busy young men and girls rush about, flitting from floor to floor and from door to door, pencils behind their ears and stuck in their hair, green shades over their eyes, ink stains on their fingers. Great motor trucks are backed up under immense shelters at one end of the building, and bales of magazines are being loaded into them for transportation to railroad shipping points. Gray-clad postmen—but those fellows are entirely too reminiscent of erstwhile heartaches. I entered an elevator and asked to be let off at the editorial floor.

A pleasant-faced woman seated behind a desk in a cubbyhole at one side of a square, boxed-in room containing for furniture only a settee or two, spoke my name into a telephone transmitter. In a moment she smiled at me.

"Do you know the way over to the *Western Story* office? No?" She called, and a boy appeared. "Take this gentleman to Mr. Blackwell's office, please."

The boy conducted me through halls, down corridors, into offices from which arose the busy clatter of typewriters, up short flights of steps and down others, and finally into a big room filled with desks whose surfaces were fairly plastered with manuscripts. It was a formidable array of contributions; I recognized them instantly as such, to be sure. And they were being read by a small army of young men and women—those individuals we writers know as "readers."

Miss Strope's roll-top desk was in a corner. Miss Strope smiled at me and beckoned me to a seat beside the desk. A quietly dressed young woman is Miss Strope, with the pink glow of perfect health in her cheeks and the alert bearing of one who, despite the sedentary character of her occupation, spends much time in the open. A young woman whose intelligence shows in her eyes, her good breeding, in the dignity of her greeting. Her handclasp was firm and of unmistakable cordiality.

"It is a pleasure to have you here," she said simply.

A slender, smooth-faced man in a close-fitting brown suit appeared. He had dark, twinkling eyes and a friendly smile. It was Mr. Blackwell; and when he had been introduced he pulled up a chair, sat on one edge of it, crossed his legs and got down to business.

"We don't very often see our out-of-town authors here," he said. "Glad you came. Now—"

And he launched into a conversation relative to the needs and requirements of his three magazines, without wasting a moment. He knew what I had come to New York for and lost no time whatever in supplying me with the information. My letters from him had, as a rule, been only a paragraph or two in length. Now he talked in reams. And he talked straight to the point.

"What we want," he said, "is stories. We never have enough of them; never! I need nearly 750,000 words of fiction and fillers a month to fill my three magazines. This matter must conform to our standard, of course. And if you don't think it's a job to select 750,000 words of passable stuff every month, the year around, you ought to come into this office and see for yourself.

"Stories, stories, stories!" Mr. Blackwell threw up his hands in the gesture of one whose task is almost greater than he can bear. "It's almost a nightmare, sometimes, to get them. Every now and then I draw a long breath and say: 'Well, this number is taken care of, at last. Now I can breathe!' And then will come notice from some department, to the effect that four or five thousand words more are needed to fill a hole. We've got to start digging, hard, to fill that hole."

"You must get plenty of stories, don't you?" I suggested.

"Certainly," he said. "We get them by the bale. But we must go over them with a fine-tooth comb to get what we want. And every time we find a yarn that will fit we give a whoop of joy. This job is a perpetual search. It is endless. A prolific author, who can turn out the kind of fiction we want, is worth his weight in gold to us. Why, do you know, Street & Smith paid one author $42,900 last year? And this chap made $9000 additional in motion picture rights, that I know of—to say nothing of even more revenue he made from motion picture rights upon which I have no figures. That's how much we think of a prolific writer who has learned our requirements."

"Tell me of some of your requirements," I suggested. Mr. Blackwell scratched his head.

"Well," he said at length, "I think I may start off by saying that the principal one is—the story. It must overshadow everything else in the yarn, this thing I call 'the story.' It must take precedence over setting, description, narration, style—everything. It must grip and hold attention. It must have a valid excuse for being. It must be fundamentally sound, and susceptible of close analysis and scrutiny.

"One of our greatest tasks is to find real stories in the many contributions that are submitted. I don't think I refer to plot particularly; for a story may have an excellent plot, conforming to all technical requirements, and still fall short. It may have high-powered action, striking atmosphere, graceful narration, and authenticity, and still not be a pulsing story. Even strong characterization will not turn the trick, sometimes, despite the fact that the other elements may be present. The author must *feel* that he has a story, perhaps, before he sets a line down on paper. Often I read yarns in which I can find no flaw, yet reject them. They lack that intangible, indescribable quality I call the 'story.' They are unconvincing, mechanical, creaking with machinery. They lack spontaneity. These things would not be true if they were properly conceived in the first place.

"Next, I think I would stress the value of impression. An impression often does not particularize. There is a marked difference, you know, between an impression and an opinion. The latter may be based upon such thorough familiarity with the facts that a mere impression would not be descriptive of the actual state of mind.

"A writer, we'll say, wants to do a series of stories in a mining setting. He knows little or nothing about mines, so he travels to a mining country and proceeds to make a personal inspection. He looks over numerous specimens of ore and rock, and takes notes upon their various names and classifications, he goes through tunnels and workings. He talks with miners and picks up picturesque phrases. He talks with mining engineers and jots down bits of technical information. He emerges at the end of a week or so with several notebooks filled from cover to cover, and so much detail that when he attempts to write a story, he is bewildered. His yarn is pretty sure to be more of a textbook on phraseology and terminology than it is a real story. In other words, he has gone beyond the point of mere impression, and has loaded himself with so much detailed material he can't handle it.

"I think that it is better for a writer to pick up just what he needs for his story, and no more. Then the picture he draws is more likely to have the effect he desires it to have on the reader—the effect of a vivid impression.

"Compactness is another quality I would stress. A story may be long and still be compact and closely-knit. A loosely constructed story can always he improved by the elimination of nonessential matter. If a situation can be described in two short sentences, with no loss of, and especially with a *gain* of, vividness of impression, then the two sentences should by all means be employed instead of the more prolix method. We want compactness in our stories; for compactness often heightens vivid impression and gives us that thing we call 'the story.' "

Mr. Blackwell told me that stories which sometimes appear in the so-called higher class magazines would be refused promptly by the kind known as the "all-fiction."

"Such stories may be executed with the skill born of the experience of the writers, but they fail to measure up to the standard of compactness we set up," he explained. "They are often deliberately stretched out, in order to carry them over into the advertising pages. I know of a case where the editor of one of our most widely circulated magazines offered to buy a story from a friend of mine, provided the author would increase its length from five thousand words to nine thousand. My friend at first declared he could not do it. He insisted that he had told the whole story in the five thousand words, and that to add any more to it would constitute nothing less than mere padding. Nevertheless, the editor was urgent, and my friend reluctantly 'pulled' the yarn out until it was as thin as tissue paper, so to speak. And the editor bought it, paying a good price.

"Such a policy would never do in the print-paper magazines. Our readers are interested in the story, and in nothing else. They read to be entertained, and they are more discriminating than you might think. A padded story draws their fire immediately. Hence, the print-paper magazine fiction contributor must deliver real stories, whether he has any literary style or not. His work may be rougher, but it will have real virility."

The Street & Smith market is virtually inexhaustible and insatiable. But its editorial requirements are closely drawn, and the only way to find out what kind of material the editors want is to read their books. To the discerning reader such reading will furnish a fairly accurate index. For publishing is distinctly a business; one editor described it to me as a "science." The fellows who manufacture the magazines and sell them by the millions know what their readers want. Moreover, they keep pace with every shifting demand. Just now the Western story is in high esteem. This condition may change; when it does, you may be sure that these editors will be among the very first to know it. It is certain that they will discover the trend long before the authors do, because that is a part of their business.

One writer named by Mr. Blackwell—the one who drew down the $42,900 for his fiction last year—lives in England and turns out fiction with almost the undiminished constancy of water coming out of a hose. His copy, I was told, is hardly a model for literary typists to follow. It requires considerable editing, and when it reaches the linotype machines it looks something like the cub reporter's first story.

But it has all the elements of real fiction—action, atmosphere, alacrity of movement, characterization, virility. The characters are *alive*. The stories are compact, closely-knit. And this author is not, I was told, a young man any more. He is a veteran whose real name never appears over his work. So prolific is he that he employs three noms de plume. He receives three cents a word, straight, for everything he sells. And he sells everything he turns out.

"What we want out of an author is volume, as well as quality work," one editor told me. Mr. Blackwell did not say this in so many words, but I gathered that he feels the same way about it. "Volume," this other editor went on, "is what builds up a following for the author, and enables the editor and publisher to determine how much his work is in demand. We think a lot of the writer who works steadily, and turns out a steady stream of material."

I asked Mr. Blackwell about the availability of the long story, as compared with that of the short.

"The real money for the author is in long stories, after he has learned to write them," he said. "It takes more work to turn out the serial or novelette. It must be planned, blueprinted, in advance. More perspiration must be shed. There are certain tricks to be learned. One of them is to insert some event, early in the yarn, which overshadows the entire story to the very end. There must be more complications and complexities. Each chapter must hold a promise of interesting development in the next. Generally speaking, I should say that the difference between the long story and the short is the difference between hard work and planning, and work and planning that are not so hard. There is always a market for a good, long story."

Before I took my departure Miss Strope mentioned one of my stories, which she had rejected a short time before as being improperly developed. She agreed that certain changes in it might make it available, and together we worked out these changes. When I returned to Denver I rewrote the story, and this time it "stuck." Which is merely another evidence that a personal visit to the editor may pay in dollars and cents. It is also illustrative of the fact that editors can be of substantial aid to writers in working out their stories to fit the magazine at which it is to be aimed.

Since talking with these two outstanding members of the magazine editorial profession, I have come to the conclusion that editors know what they want, although they are not always able to take the time to put their requirements into words. I am also convinced that the best way of learning their requirements is to read their magazines, and *study* the stories printed therein. This means more than mere casual perusal. It means analysis, the application of logic and reason.

You will learn, for instance, that Mr. Blackwell prefers stories with few characters, and with the actions of the dominant character followed closely all the way through; that profanity is absolutely taboo; that a situation in which a woman is being mistreated will not be tolerated; that only one set of characters is wanted; that strength of plot is desirable, but that characterization is even more so; that *sympathetic* characterization always gets under the editorial skin; that convincingness is the pearl of great price; that plausibility must never be sacrificed, under any circumstances; and that it is mighty hard to sell him a short story of more than 6000 words, no matter what he says about "no limit on length." I have no doubt but that he would buy a longer short story, provided he could find one that bore no evidences of padding. But how often does that happen?

[*The Author & Journalist*, October 1926]

Meeting the Editors in Person
Harry E. Maule, A.H. Bittner, Anthony M. Rud

[Though he had deep experience as an editor, Anthony Melville Rud (1893-1942) is better known as a fictioneer. In fact, he's probably doomed to be best-remembered as the author of the immortal "Ooze," since it graced the cover of the first issue of *Weird Tales* (March 1923) in two-color glory. But by that time, his career was well underway. He graduated from Dartmouth in 1914. In a February 1939 article for *Writer's Digest*, Rud claimed to have sold a series of eight detective stories to editor Ray Long at *Red Book* in 1915. His memory proved quite inaccurate in the article so dates can't be certain, but Long jumped ship to start his celebrated run at *Cosmopolitan* in late-'18, so that sets the limit. Rud's first editorial job was with *Illustrated World*, a non-fiction magazine, to which he also supplied a number of articles. The article dates range from August '15 to January '18. His fiction career picks up after that. Though he placed a short in *The Saturday Evening Post* (August 23, 1919), after that his fiction output was almost exclusively pulp through the rest of his life. His next editing job was *West*, under Harry Maule at Doubleday, a job which lasted from early-'26 through late-'27. He made numerous fiction sales to Doubleday at the same time, to *Frontier* and *Short Stories*. Around September '27, Rud moved over to Butterick to edit *Adventure*. The date of this switch coincides with the merger of Doubleday, Page with the George H. Doran Company to form Doubleday, Doran, though there's no evidence of a connection to Rud's departure. While at Butterick, the ill-fated *Everybody's* and *Romance* came into his editorial orbit. Rud was out at Butterick after January 1930, which led to a lull in his career. The early years of the Depression were tough on freelance writers, but Rud's problems may have been compounded by persistent alcoholism. In the 1939 article, he fondly reminisced: "The only time I ever spent an evening with Hammett, he and I drank two bottles apiece of Bushmill's Irish Whiskey which had been given to me by [writer and critic] Burton Rascoe. Hammett did not even recognize me when I met him in the lobby of the Ambassador a day later. That was all right. I couldn't recognize him, either." An ad in the April 1930 *Writer's Digest* heralded in big letters: Write For the Billion-Word Market. The advertiser was the Popular Fiction Institute. "Specialized instruction by eight successful editor-authors will help you make rapid progress," they promised. Rud's name was listed, alongside other well-known editors like A.H. Bittner, A.A. Wyn, and Eugene A. Clancy. The venture didn't last long, and probably didn't pay much. By 1932, Rud's fictioneering was back in full-flower. His name appeared in a variety of pulps, especially *Detective Fiction Weekly* and *Argosy*. In late '37, it was back to an editor's desk, this time *Detective Story* and *Clues*. This lasted until the summer of 1939, when he left Street & Smith, replaced by his assistant, Hazlett Kessler. In 1942, Rud died of a heart attack, age 49. :: These notes are indebted to Peter Ruber's on-line article, "Anthony

M. Rud." (pulprack.com) :: Notes on Maule and Bittner accompany their respective *Editors You Want To Know* profiles.]

ANY WRITER WHO SUFFERS from the hallucination that magazine publishing falls short of being a business, in any particular, should make a pilgrimage to New York and conduct a first-hand investigation. He will discover, among other things, that the editor who is not a businessman as well as an editor has no permanent or important place in the magazine manufacturing industry. I am speaking, please understand, of that class of magazines known variously as "popular," "print paper," "pulp," "all-fiction," etc. The kind that sell for from ten to twenty-five cents a copy and depend almost altogether upon virile fiction appeal for their sales, and upon those sales for the major part of their income.

Out at Garden City, Long Island, the famous publishing plant of Doubleday, Page & Company is one of the showplaces of that beautiful little city. Your railroad ticket reads "Country Life Press," which is the name of the station at which you alight. Three-quarters of an hour are consumed on the journey from the Pennsylvania station in New York. When you arrive you find it difficult to realize that the teeming metropolis of nearly seven-million people—not all of them authors, either—is only a few miles away. For Garden City is a place of wide streets, spacious lawns, beautiful trees and all the other things that go to make up a community of real homes.

The big publishing plant covers acres, and is surrounded by groves, lawns and flowerbeds. Great stone steps lead into the high-ceilinged reception hall. A girl at a desk labeled "information" directed me to a huge room flanking the reception hall, and began manipulating the switchboard before her. In the room designated, I sank into a luxuriously upholstered divan and wondered what the editor would do to the contributor exhibiting the colossal nerve to call for an interview. I really felt as if I might be committing lese majesty in invading this temple of luxury.

But I needn't have feared. In a few minutes a smiling young man came in and looked me over. He held out his hand.

"I'm Bittner," he said.

A.H. Bittner, associate editor, whose particular charge is *The Frontier* magazine! I had sold him a thing or two, and corresponded with him a lot. I had read his excellent articles in THE AUTHOR & JOURNALIST. It may surprise him to know that I stood somewhat in awe of him. And here he was, a boyish figure, either very glad to see me or else simulating gladness with consummate art. He sat down by my side and we began to talk.

When I began to fire questions at him, however, he stopped me.

"Wait until I get Mr. Maule. He'll tell you everything you want to know."

In two or three minutes he was back, with Harry E. Maule in tow. Mr. Maule is favorably known to thousands of writers for his friendly criticisms, his informative letters and his system of developing writers who interest him professionally. He knows how to throw a note of real cordiality into even the briefest missives. He is delightfully informal in his correspondence, even with writers to him unknown. He directs his corps of associate and assistant editors with a skillful hand. Despite his numerous duties and activities as an important directing editorial head, he finds time to travel west occasionally, and to get into intimate touch with the land that figures so largely in the stories at least two of his magazines print.

Mr. Maule is a slender chap whose dark hair is beginning to show threads of gray. In speech he is incisive. I missed the familiar "New York accent," and in a moment knew why. He told me that he was raised in Denver and educated in the West. He asked me about one or two of his old friends in that city.

"I'm coming out West this summer," he remarked after a few minutes' conversation. "Going to join a pack train in Montana."

I recalled that Mr. Maule has often taken his summer vacation in Colorado and other Western states. For several minutes we talked of these things. Then we took up the business that had brought me to New York.

Mr. Maule likes his stories to be authentic and "close to the ground," he told me. Being a Western man, he knows what "close to the ground" is. He likes accuracy of detail in stories he buys for his magazines. There must be something more than mere action, plot, atmosphere, characterization. The story must ring true, be convincing and be susceptible of the closest scrutiny with reference to geographical, historical and technical detail. One look at the keen eyes and countenance of this editor tells the observant interviewer that he is a businessman in every sense of the word, with a really extraordinary power of perception.

It is not hard to understand why Mr. Maule insists upon authenticity in the stories he purchases for publication. Being a businessman, he watches very carefully the reactions of his readers. Subscribers in the cow country, for instance, are exceedingly quick to detect an inaccuracy of detail in a story— and many of them are equally quick to write in and tell the editor about it.

For instance, a cowboy once said to me:

"Whatever yuh do, don't ever have any cowpuncher in yore stories make camp by th' side of a crick, or in a draw. Sometime in th' night there's liable to be a cloudburst up in th' mountains, an' yore puncher'll wake up to find himself plumb drowned!"

It is this sort of thing that Mr. Maule insists shall be kept in mind for his stories. The holster must be worn on the proper side of the character's body; no cowboy is allowed to mount his "hoss" from the wrong side; a rodeo must be described with an eye to fact; gold must be discovered in the right kind of formation; cowboy "lingo" must he in accordance with the speech of the particular part of the West in which the story lies, and so on.

But there is another thing required by Mr. Maule of his contributors, if the best results are to be obtained for both writer and editor. That is "volume."

"Volume of output is essential to the building up of a following for any author," he said. "An occasional story in any one magazine by a writer will not accomplish this end. The writer's value to the magazine is determined by the size and character of his following—the number of readers who like his work, buy the magazine partly because of it, and let us know how they feel about it.

"This end is not usually attained by submitting stories to a wide variety of magazines. Perhaps the author may take pride in seeing his name in the tables of contents of a dozen or more magazines; but unless he is extraordinarily prolific, he is not as a rule building up a following in any one of those publications. Hence the editor cannot gauge his value as evidenced by the approval or disapproval of any considerable number of his magazine's readers."

This brought up a point about which I had always been puzzled.

"How do you ascertain the feelings of readers about an author's work?" I asked. "Do you receive enough voluntary letters from them to sound the general attitude?"

Mr. Maule smiled.

"Well," he replied, "magazine publishing, you understand, is a science. We have been in the business a great many years, and in that time we have learned many ways of gauging the reaction of readers to any single issue.

"Our circulation representatives, for instance, are scattered all over the country. It is their business, among other duties, to check this reaction. They talk with the owners of newsstands and the managers of central news distributing agencies. They gather up a lot of information relative to how such and such an issue was received; what comments have been caught relative to the stories printed therein; why certain issues have not sold as well as previous ones, or vice versa.

"It is quite common for the circulation of a magazine to fluctuate by thousands of copies. One number may be several thousand below another in sales. Or it may be several thousand above. There are times when we have extraordinary drops, or jumps, in circulation; and naturally a variety of reasons are assigned. Many times these reasons have to do with the reading matter; a new serial by a popular author, for instance, whose name is printed on the cover, may shoot the sales skyward.

"The fact that the author has a following is responsible. Readers have read his stuff and like it. The mere announcement that he is in the table of contents will create a demand for the magazine. That is why I stress the importance of volume in an author's output. He is a highly important factor in the financial success of the publication."

Mr. Maule also pointed out the importance of volume of output as a factor, in rate of payment.

The larger his output of acceptable material, the larger the word rate he may command from the treasurer's office, Mr. Maule implied. The occasional contributor may be in no position to demand an advanced rate since he has no definite following in that magazine. When he has demonstrated his worth, however, from a reader-demand standpoint, the editor is likely to raise his rate voluntarily. He must first demonstrate his pulling power as a box-office attraction; otherwise he must content himself with a rate of compensation somewhere near the minimum.

The titles of Mr. Maule's three magazines tell the story of their separate requirements in a fiction way, with reasonable clarity. *Short Stories* wants short stories of adventure, novelettes, serials. They may be laid in the West or anywhere else where adventures are had. *The Frontier* and *West* both use Western stories, but those in *West* are more of the rollicking cowboy type than those in *The Frontier*.

Mr. Bittner takes a genuine, enthusiastic interest in writers and their wares. He is a young man of demonstrated capability in choosing the right stories for his magazine. He loves a good story as some men love their wives. When he buys, his letter of acceptance inevitably reflects the joy he has experienced at once more discovering "pay dirt." He can get as excited over a thrilling situation in a story as a debutante over her first coming-out party.

You will never lose, gentle writer, by taking infinite pains with a story you purpose submitting to Bittner. He has a keen appreciation of painstaking work, and never forgets to let you know it. If he can send you a check, he does so with almost hilarious satisfaction. I don't mean that he is easy to sell; far from it. He is an excellent judge of a good story, and a story must be pretty good to get by him. But once the yarn has passed the test, Bittner is almost ready to fall on your neck for letting him buy it.

Owing to a luncheon engagement in New York I had to cut my visit short. Mr. Bittner escorted me clear to the depot, and as the train was pulling out, shouted:

"I'll be looking for your stuff!"

On the way out I was introduced fleetingly to Anthony Rud, the author-editor of *West*, whose stories appear with considerable frequency in other magazines. Mr. Rud's huge hand completely enclosed mine as we shook hands. He has the tonnage displacement of a football star, and, like Bittner, he is young. There is only one other editor on earth who approaches him in avoirdupois, so far as I know, and that is Arthur E. Scott, editor of *Top-Notch* of the Street & Smith publications. Not fat, mind you; just big. And both mighty capable editors.

Mr. Bittner took me through the vast Doubleday-Page basement on the way to the depot, as a short-cut. It looks to cover about five acres, although of course it is not so large as that; and it is literally jammed with millions of books, all neatly covered with paper. I gasped when I saw them.

"What do you intend to do with all these books?" I demanded. There were enough to fill two or three gross of ordinary Carnegie libraries, it seemed to me.

"Sell 'em," Bittner replied with a grin. "What did you suppose?"

A look at that immense stock of books would bolster up the waning hopes of any discouraged author. If one publishing concern can do business on such a mammoth scale, the demand for material from writers must almost exceed the powers of calculation of expert mathematicians. And to see the truckloads of magazines snorting away from the plant—trucks piled as high as old-fashioned loads of hay—cannot fail to impress any observer with the magnitude of this vast industry. Someone has estimated that about ten million story manuscripts find their way into the editorial offices of New York magazines annually, of which a goodly number are sent winging back to their creators with more or less promptness; nevertheless, consideration of the huge bulk of business done by the publishing companies will give rise to the query:

Anthony Rud

"What would become of the business if all the writers were to quit?"

The kindness shown me by Mr. Maule and his associates strengthened the conviction that most editors believe in encouraging the author, however insignificant he may be. For I am just one of the little fellows. In the rank and file of the army of writers I am a mere private, a "doughboy," hardly more than a raw recruit. Many a rejection comes my way, accompanied by a jovially sarcastic letter—or even by a rejection slip. Is this the best I can do?

Call on a few New York editors of the caliber of those I have thus far described, and note the change that takes place in your consciousness. Heretofore, you have been sending stories to "institutions," manned by vague personalities whose printed rejections or cold, one-line letters declining your wares may have had the effect of a shower of cold rain upon your writing enthusiasm.

From now on, however, you are sending your stories to live, keen individuals who know your problems as well as you know them yourself, and who are as anxious to see you succeed as even you could possibly be. If they have never told you so, it is because they literally haven't had the time.

Take my word for it!

[*The Author & Journalist*, November 1926]

Meeting the Editors in Person
Matthew White, Jr., Robert Simpson, Richard A. Martinsen

[In 1885, Matthew White, Jr. (1857-1940) started *Boy's Work* magazine. Two years later, he sold it to Frank A. Munsey and joined Munsey's editorial staff. Just after *The Golden Argosy* simplified its title to *The Argosy* (December 1988), White became full editor of the magazine. With the October '96 issue, *The Argosy* went to all-fiction making it the first pulp, and White the first pulp editor. He remained editor of *Argosy*, under its various title changes, until his retirement in May 1928 at the age of 70, when A.H. Bittner took over. His reign of four decades presiding over a single magazine, and a very successful one at that, puts him in the pantheon of the great editors of the pulps. If that were not enough, for twenty-eight years he was dramatic editor of *Munsey's*. He also wrote short stories and serials for the Munsey publications, and published several novels. :: Born in Strathy, Scotland, Robert Simpson (1886-1934) grew up in Glasgow. At 19, he went to West Africa—the White Man's Grave, as it was known by visitors. "I had the job of putting up the new wharf; that is, the Kroo-boys did the work while I stood around looking white and anxious. But my greatest achievement on the Coast was a concrete breakwater or river wall. I didn't know anything about concrete or foundations or tides or Niger mud or anything like that when I began. And I don't know anything about 'em now—except the mud." He moved to the United States in 1907 and soon his stories began appearing in pulp magazines, *The Cavalier*, *All-Story*. In 1910, *All-Story* began running his serials, sometimes overlapping two at once (employing a pseudonym, Simeon Robertson). He joined the editorial staff of The Frank A. Munsey Company in 1916, and his publication record goes blank. The following year, he became managing editor of *The Argosy*, presumably as Matthew White's subordinate. White had spent time in London (ca. 1913-14) as Munsey's literary representaive, and Simpson's editorship may represent White's further disengagement from the hand's-on duties. Simpson remained in the position for three years. Thereafter, through the mid-'20s, he devoted himself to freelancing, appearing in *Adventure* and *Everybody's*, and writing novels. His Niger Delta experience formed the basis of much of his work. *Mystery Magazine* was revived in January 1926 (after a year's hiatus) with Simpson onboard as editor, a job he held for almost two years before returning to freelancing. The end of his life was marred by a two-year illness that rendered him an invalid. With the publication of his last story in *Adventure* (March 1934), this was noted in The Camp-Fire: "In keeping with old custom, and in keeping with the emotions engendered by the passing of a comrade, we pause for a moment to mark the death of Robert Simpson, one of the Old Guard of the Writers' Brigade." :: Notes on Martinsen accompany "What In Thunder *Is* Their Policy?"]

BEFORE I WENT TO NEW YORK on this editor-interviewing trip I had a very inadequate idea of the indescribable vastness of our metropolis, in spite of all I had read and heard about it.

For instance, I thought that the job of visiting the editors would be a comparatively simple one, involving at most a brisk saunter from one magazine office to another. I knew that most of the big theatres of Manhattan were in one district, and I suppose I had the impression that all the publishing houses were similarly in close proximity to each other.

Believe me, they are not! The Street & Smith plant, for instance, located at 79-89 Seventh Avenue, is so far away from most of the other publishing establishments that an airplane could very profitably be used in getting from one to the other, provided there were any place to land. Fiction House, Inc. is about the nearest to it, being only four or five miles farther up the island of Manhattan. Then to get to the headquarters of the Clayton Publications, from which emanate *Ace-High Magazine, Cowboy Stories*, etc., one must trek across the city from 461 Eighth avenue (the address of Fiction House) to 799 Broadway, a considerable distance even as the crow flies. And there are no crows flying about New York City.

Everybody who has ever sold a story or who is trying to sell one knows about Robert H. "Bob" Davis. Now please don't get excited; I must confess right at the outset that I failed to see the notable Bob. He wasn't in New York at the time. But I conscientiously tried to see him; for Bob bought my first story, back in the early winter of 1917, and gave me encouragement to hope that someday I might actually become, an author. Thereafter he bought a whole series of stories from me, and I very definitely suspect that he was the only editor in the whole wide world that would have fooled with me at that early stage of my development. All hail to Bob Davis!

"Two-eighty Broadway" is what the Frank A. Munsey Company inscribes upon its embossed stationery as its New York editorial address.

"That," I said to myself, "means that it is in the 300-block on Broadway. I am now in the 1100-block. Ergo, I have only eight blocks to go. I might as well walk."

I started out. About an hour and three quarters later I paused in front of an ornate department store show window and took stock. The number over the main entrance of the department store was "967." How was this thus?

And then, belatedly, I remembered what Editor Hawkins of THE AUTHOR & JOURNALIST had told me before I started from Denver. "New York," he said, "does not number its streets one hundred to the block. It clings to the old fashioned plan of straight, consecutive numbering, without reference to blocks."

So, I took a Broadway surface car. Just why New Yorkers ride the surface cars is an unfathomable mystery. Held up by crosstown traffic at every street intersection, the progress of a surface car in New York would put the proverbial snail to shame. Walking is twice as rapid, in addition to which the pedestrian does not have to suffer the terrific jolts he is certain to encounter when he rides the surface car. I remained on this one a half hour or so, and then discovered that I had arrived at seven-hundred-and-something! I left the car flat on its back and stood on a street corner for a spell, trying to piece my scattered wits together.

Two-eighty Broadway, it was evident, was a long, long ways off yet. It was equally evident that ordinary means of transportation would not get me there that day. Should I hail one of the innumerable taxicabs that dashed down Broadway? Or should I walk a couple of blocks eastward and take an elevated?

I decided upon the latter. I might have taken a subway; but for the stranger the New York subway is an adventure. You don't know where you are, and you don't know where the subway train is going. It may land you up in the Bronx when you thought you were headed for Battery Park. On the elevated you can at least view the passing scenery. If you don't see Central Park in the course of your ride, you may be reasonably certain that you are at least headed in the right direction.

I was to make another discovery. New York street numbers do not parallel each other. That is, a certain number on one street will not approximate a similar number on a parallel street. I alighted when the train was in the three-hundreds—and when I had walked over to Broadway I discovered that so far as that thoroughfare was concerned I had progressed only so far as the five-hundreds!

By this time I was desperate. I would find two-eighty if I had to spend the night in a hotel en route. So I walked, sturdily and with set jaws, down twisting Broadway, between skyscrapers that grew in height by leaps and bounds, until I finally came to a pause before an arched entrance having over it the words: "The Sun." The number, I noted, was "280."

I had started at a reasonably early hour in the morning, and it was now after one in the afternoon. An elevator discharged me, footsore and weary, at the floor where the Munsey editorial offices are located. A pretty little black-haired, brown-eyed miss informed me that Mr. Davis was not in; that Mr. Titherington of *Munsey's* magazine, to whom I had sold a couple of stories, was also out, but that I might see Mr. White if I desired.

Matthew White, Jr.! Who hasn't heard of him? Or who, among the writing fraternity, has not at some time received one of his kindly letters? 'Way back in 1915, I recall, he returned one of my efforts with a letter something like this:

"If your story had been one-half as clever as the letter you sent with it, I would have been delighted to send you a check therefore. As it is—" etc.

To which I replied:

"Well, I see you kept the letter. Why not send me a check for *it?*"

I had read Mr. White's clever play reviews for many years. I recalled when his name used to be emblazoned on the old *Argosy*, then a bright yellow as to cover, the only all-fiction magazine in the country. He must be incredibly ancient by now, I reflected. A moment later the brown-eyed miss was showing me into his office.

A dapper little man was seated at a plain, flat-topped desk at one side of a plainly-furnished room whose broad windows looked out on the roofs and incomparable skyline of lower Manhattan. He had gray hair, modishly cut and carefully brushed, and an almost-white mustache of military trimness. His eyes—no, I can't for the life of me remember their color, unless they are gray—had the snap and sparkle of a boy of twenty as he rose, held out his hand and bade me welcome.

"Sit down, sir," he said formally. "What can I do for you?"

Matthew White, Jr.

I informed him that he could tell me a few things if he were so inclined. Some way or other, that plainly furnished office didn't look like any arena for mere foolishness. Mr. White tempered its severity, to be sure, but I had a hunch that I had better get to the business that brought me here, as quickly and expeditiously as possible.

"I never sold a story to you," I said, "but I used to sell quite a lot to Bob Davis."

One should never, by any chance, refer to that $25,000-a-year editor as anything but "Bob." It denotes a familiarity with greatness that, in turn, spells presumed ease in its presence. "He bought my first story, in fact."

Mr. White laughed. "Bob has bought a good many maiden efforts, in his time," he said.

"He started me out as an author," I said.

"He has started a lot of them," Mr. White came back at me.

I hastened to give a different slant to the conversation. Clearly it is no distinction to have been discovered by Bob Davis. He has, through a long career as an editor, developed a habit of discovering authors.

I asked Mr. White something about his requirements, as compared with those of Mr. Davis. The latter, be it remembered, was for years the managing editor of all the Munsey magazine publications, and had the *All-Story* magazine as his especial charge.

Now that he has retired from magazine editorship and is devoting himself mainly to writing a column for *The Sun*, Mr. White has become the chief manuscript purchaser for the combined *Argosy All-Story*.

Mr. White's requirements, it appeared, are considerably different from those of his predecessor.

"I don't want to get the reputation of being an easy editor to sell to," he said. "I would rather be known as an editor to whom it is hard to sell stories. To get into the columns of this magazine is not easy for the average writer, these days. I require yarns bearing evidences of extreme care, in the preparation of them—and yarns, in addition, that violate the traditions relative to 'logical development.'

"By this I mean that I do not want the story developed in what is commonly called the 'natural way.' I require *unexpected* development—surprises at every turn it is possible to have them without destroying the convincingness of the story. I don't want stories so easily developed that the writer has only to say to himself: 'This is what would naturally follow at this point,' and proceed to write out that development.

"In other words," Mr. White concluded, "stories that are a constant challenge to the author's inventive ability, one situation after another, and that keep the writer perspiring freely. That is what I want in the *Argosy All-Story*."

So there you are. I have no doubt but that Mr. White sticks to his theory, too; for I haven't yet sold him a thing, although recently he wrote me that he would have bought a certain story from me had the solution of my problem been more convincing.

"Mr. Munsey's motto, kept constantly dangling before the eyes of his editorial staff, was 'Good, easy reading,' " Mr. White wrote. "Your ending might be convincing to readers living in Colorado, where the scene of your story is laid; but I am afraid that in other parts of the country it would only puzzle folks."

There is no set of magazines more prompt with editorial checks than the Munsey group. The decisions of its editors are prompt and irrevocable. It has been my experience that it seldom pays to rewrite a rejected story, in whole or in part, and expect to sell to them. Likewise, I believe it a waste of time to send them stories rejected by other editors; although, of course, there are exceptions to all rules. I merely state my individual experience.

At the Munsey offices I learned that Robert Simpson, for many years the editor of the old *Argosy*, had taken that position with the *Mystery Magazine*, whose editorial offices are in the St. James building, 1100 Broadway. Mr. Simpson had purchased several stories from me in the old days, therefore I straightway hied myself back up that long, diagonally-traveling artery—this time taking a means of transportation that would get me there before dark. I found Mr. Simpson to be a handsome gentleman of middle age, inclined to fall back upon a Scottish accent during emphatic moments, and able to set forth clearly and unmistakably his requirements for the magazine he is directing. For a minute or two we talked of the days when he used to buy my stories for *Argosy* and particularly of his kindly interest in the struggles of a neophyte in this difficult game. I recalled to his mind that he had once purchased a story from me after its seventh or eighth revision as to climax. Once he wrote advising me to "let this yarn lie fallow for six months or so, until it acquires a punch." I followed his advice, and six months to the day I resurrected the story, read it over, saw where I had got off the track and rewrote the ending. Mr. Simpson retorted with a check by return mail.

Robert Simpson's last appearance in *Adventure*

As I spoke of these things now he laughed.

"Why don't you write some stories for me now?" he asked. I looked my horror.

"What—me write a mystery story?" (Lapses in grammar are by no means infrequent even in a New York editorial office.) "I never wrote a mystery story in my life. I wouldn't know how to begin one."

Mr. Simpson laid a fatherly hand on my shoulder. Not that I am so much younger than he; to tell the truth, I am several years older. But he appears to be that kind of an editor.

"My boy," he said impressively, "any good story may be a mystery story. When you get back home, I want you to try something for me."

"All right," I responded. "As soon as I get home I'll get a copy of your magazine and read it over—"

"What for?" he interrupted.

"Why, so as to get some idea of what kind of stories you want!"

"Don't do it," Mr. Simpson fairly ordered. "Don't, by any means, do it! I don't want you to *look* at the magazine until after you have written and mailed me your story."

Well, I failed to obey his orders. When I returned to Denver, in due course I bought a copy of *Mystery Magazine* and read it from cover to cover. When I had finished I took a plot I had had in my head for some time and wrote the yarn.

"This will hit Simpson as sure as I'm a foot high," I told my wife. "It's a mystery, and I have written it in the general style of the stories he's running."

I mailed it, and sat back to wait for the check, accompanied by Simpson's grateful letter of appreciation. Instead, in a disconcertingly short time back came the story. It wouldn't do. I rewrote it and submitted it again. Same thing. Three times I sent Simpson that mystery yarn, and three times it came back. Then I gave up. Some day, when I have completely forgotten every story I read in the magazine, I am going to try again!

Readers of THE AUTHOR & JOURNALIST had the pleasure of reading an article, not long ago, from the pen of Richard A. Martinsen—pronounced, by the way, "Mar*teen*son"—setting forth some of the editorial requirements of the magazines published by Fiction House, Inc. ["From Writer Into Editor," July 1926] These include *Action Stories*, *The Lariat*, *Northwest Stories* and *Love Romances*.

I called on Mr. Martinsen during my stay in New York, and was his guest at luncheon at the Pennsylvania Hotel. A dignified waiter weighing not less than two hundred and thirty pounds served us, pouring our coffee out of a silver pot with an impressively long snout. A feeling of awe creeps over me yet when I think of the size of that check; I caught a glimpse of it as my host paid the bill. What that waiter did to one of Mr. Martinsen's crisp ten-dollar bills was a shame.

AUTHOR & JOURNALIST readers know Mr. Martinsen's requirements, from reading his excellent and clear-cut article. (If Mr. Martinsen doesn't buy my next story, after this boost, he isn't properly appreciative.) He said a few things to me that did not appear in the article. He is the authors' contact man with Fiction House, by the way. It is his job to meet 'em when they come to New York, and thus relieve Mr. "Jack" Kelly, the editor-in-chief, of the job. Anyhow, Mr. Kelly was in Europe when I visited New York.

"We editors know perfectly well that the 'Old West' doesn't exist any more," he said. "And so does the average reader of Western stories, I believe. We're not fooling anybody when we publish stories setting forth the West as it used to be, presumably, and trying to give the impression that this same old West actually exists today. They all know better.

"But it is our job to keep alive the romance of it. That is what the readers want. How can it be done successfully save in graphically written stories? Life is pretty humdrum for a lot of folks these days. They are constantly seeking surcease from the monotony of existence and a lot of them find it in reading our stories of a colorful West. Whether such a West actually exists makes no difference to them. It exists for them in fiction, anyway."

Mr. Martinsen, by the way, is of the younger school of editors. He hasn't been out of Stanford University so very many years. He is a businessman as well as an editor, who keeps an eye on such things as "distribution costs," etc. When he fares forth from his office he hangs a cane over his left arm, like a bred-in-the-bone New Yorker; but in reality he is a Western product. He has big teeth and a big smile which is seldom out of commission, and when he talks he talks right to the point.

He likes to get personal letters from writers. "It relieves the monotony," he explained. "When an editor reads over story after story, day after day, he is glad to receive an occasional snappy letter to make him forget the routine. At least I am, and I think the other men on our staff are."

Fiction House offices are on the umpty-umpth floor of a huge office skyscraper; you get off at the twenty-seventh floor, or something like that, and walk down a long corridor until you reach a heavy, unwindowed door bearing the label of the publishing house. It is a busy place, as a plant publishing four teeming magazines is liable to be. But Mr. Martinsen is the soul of cordiality, full of fine suggestions and eager for material. He has many personal friends among authors, and his needs are definite.

"I do considerable writing myself," he said. "And I have found that it pays to plan out a story in advance, section by section, page by page. Also, it pays to study the magazine to which you plan to submit your yarn—study it carefully and painstakingly! That is my method, and it works beautifully. Writers who do this with relation to the Fiction House publications are succeeding, too."

I called at the editorial offices of *Adventure* that same day; but of this more anon.

[*The Author & Journalist*, December 1926]

Meeting the Editors in Person
Adventure and *Everybody's*, Arthur E. Scott, and Harold Hersey

[Arthur E. Scott joined Street & Smith about 1913, serving as associate editor on *Top-Notch* under Henry Wilton Thomas, the original editor of the magazine (under the name "Burt L. Standish," the pseudonym associated with the Frank Merriwell novels). In late-'23, Thomas retired to live in Italy and Scott took control of the magazine. Here's how he was described in the May 1922 *The Student Writer* (the original title of *Author & Journalist*): "Arthur E. Scott . . . writes poetry on the side and—murmur it low—plays rather a canny poker hand. He is only six feet seven in his stocking feet." Stone seems even more impressed with Scott's loftiness. But what impressed Scott was volume: "Judging by the mass of manuscripts that comes to my desk every morning, and considering that every editor I have met has a similar quantity, I have come to the conclusion that at least seventy-five per cent of the people of the United States are trying to write fiction." The mass of copy complemented Scott's ideal of writing: "That old adage, 'Slow and Sure,' is all wrong. Rather it should be 'Swift and Sure.' It is a scientific fact that students in school who answer questions quickly also are the most accurate. The best typist writes rapidly. The writer who succeeds is the one who writes swiftly and surely." It's doubtful Scott ever put this theory to the test himself. His own publishing record consists mostly of a scattering of poems in *Top-Notch* prior to his becoming editor; and a half-dozen short articles in *Author & Journalist* between August '26 and January '29. Ironically, he left Street & Smith just as this *Meeting the Editors in Person* series concluded, with George Briggs Jenkins succeeding him as editor of *Top-Notch*. Scott's departure may have been due to his failure to sustain the great success of *Top-Notch*, which never recovered from Thomas' retirement. In 1928, Scott started advertising himself as an "Authors' Agent and Editorial Critic," and that's essentially the last we know of him. :: For detailed information on the heralded career of Harold Hersey, we simply refer you to *The New Pulpwood Editor* (Adventure House, 2002).]

I CAN'T SAY TRUTHFULLY that I received any immediate practical benefit from my visit to the editorial offices of *Adventure* magazine, toward the end of my stay in New York City. I gathered, in fact, that *Adventure's* policy rather discourages personal visits from authors, although it is entirely possible that I am mistaken in this assumption. However, as I had been warned by another editor that "they're hard to see, those people," said editor being a chap who writes stories pretty frequently himself, I think I am safe in stating that *Adventure* as a usual thing prefers to deal with its contributors by mail.

The Butterick Publishing Company, which is responsible for *Adventure, Everybody's, The Delineator,* and the famous Butterick patterns, is housed in a tall, old-fashioned office building at the corner of Spring and MacDougal streets, toward the lower end of the island of Manhattan.

It is perhaps the most isolated of all the magazine offices in New York; at least it seemed so to me, a stranger who found it easier to get lost in the great metropolis than to find a given address. Moreover, its surroundings suggest anything but the publishing business. Apparently it is in one of the city's vast wholesale districts, the adjoining structures being given over to lofts, and warehouses, the narrow, crooked streets teeming with population of the most heterogeneous kind.

As I recall it, the *Adventure* editorial offices are on the ninth floor. A stately moving elevator, manned by an elderly man, carried me thither. I stepped forth into a long room, and a young woman at a desk inquired my business. I told her that I craved speech with one Arthur Sullivant Hoffman, editor of *Adventure*.

But Mr. Hoffman, it appeared, was out of the city. This was just a few days after the purchase of the Butterick company by new interests. Several other gentlemen whose names had been signed, at sundry times, to letters I had received from the magazine, were equally unavailable for personal interview. Finally the lady suggested that "Mr. Cox" was in and might see me.

Mr. Cox came in a few minutes. We stood at the side of a desk and talked; or, rather, I did. Mr. Cox had little to say, beyond answering my questions courteously and briefly. I found myself curiously tongue-tied. Many things I had wanted to know I failed to find out, for the simple reason, I suspect, that I forgot to ask about them. Mr. Cox was kindly and cordial, but there was that in the atmosphere which seemed to suggest, unmistakably, that I was taking up somebody's valuable time. It is an uncomfortable feeling. The time of an editor is certainly more valuable than that of a casual visitor.

Up to that time I had sold just one story to *Adventure*, and now that I think of it, the manner of its acceptance and purchase indicated a system that spelled the elimination of waste of time at every angle. The letter of acceptance was a printed form, with spaces left for filling in such items as the name of the story, suggested changes and corrections, etc. I give you my word, I didn't know I had sold a story at first. It was fully five minutes after opening the envelope that my good fortune dawned upon me; and even then I had to submit the whole proposition to a friend, and get his affirmative opinion, before I could be convinced.

The letter stated that *Adventure's* editors do not make changes in an author's manuscript without first notifying the author. They prefer to let him do it himself. I was invited, as I discovered from further perusal of this and subsequent form communications, to contribute something to "The Camp-Fire," that meeting place between authors and readers; to copyright my yarn if I cared to; to read galley proofs on it, so as to catch any errors that might have crept in; and to do other things the nature of which I have forgotten. For a long time after selling that yarn I was receiving other form letters, acquainting me with *Adventure* activities I had not dreamed of. The check was a generous one, inscribed on paper so stiff that it would stand alone; and when the story finally was printed, two copies of the magazine came to me with the editor's compliments.

Adventure had gone back to the two-a-month-plan a short time before I went to New York, and announcements sent to contributors revealed that there would be a consequent let-up in purchases for some time to come. I asked Mr. Cox about this.

"Things are just beginning to loosen up," he said. "We are starting to buy again."

And that, virtually, was all I learned from my visit. After all, I reflected, the editors of *Adventure* have for years gone to more trouble to keep contributors informed of their needs, perhaps, than almost any other magazine in the country. Personal interviews seem superfluous, when you come right down to it. No magazine is more prompt in answering inquiries by mail, and readings of manuscripts are thorough and conscientious. What is there to tell the author who calls personally?

In this connection I might add that since the announcement of a change of policy for *Everybody's* by virtue of which that magazine, beginning with the December issue, will be an all-fiction magazine similar to *Adventure*, a story which I had submitted to *Adventure*, following my visit, was accepted by the editor of *Everybody's*. In his letter of acceptance Mr. Oscar Graeve, editor, said: "Your story did not quite make the grade with *Adventure* and was turned over to me for consideration for *Everybody's*. I like it a lot and enclose," etc. That seems to mean that manuscripts submitted to either magazine will be considered by both.

On the way back up town I dropped in again at the Street & Smith offices and asked to see Arthur E. Scott, editor of *Top-Notch*. There was something about which I desired to consult Mr. Scott. I had never sold him anything—have not even yet, for that matter—but I had hopes.

He came out to the reception room in response to my message. Mr. Scott is, as I have stated before in this series, a very large man as to up-and-down measurements. Horizontally speaking, he is about average. How he missed being commandeered for the New York police force is a mystery to me; for the New York police commissioners take pride in having some of the biggest, as well as the handsomest, policemen in the world. Mr. Scott would meet all requirements as to both size and pulchritude. And yet, for all his bulk, he writes a hand so small and fine that it is the envy and despair of most feminine chirographists.

"Suppose," I asked Mr. Scott, "I send a story to one of the Street & Smith magazines, and it is rejected. Is there any chance that any of the other Street & Smith editors might buy that yarn, if they knew of its previous rejection?"

"There is just as good a chance to sell it as though it had come straight to the second editor in the first place," he assured me.

And then he cited a case in point:

"A New York author brought two stories to me recently," he said. "I read them over, and they didn't make the grade. So I returned them.

"A week or two later he came in and informed me that he had sold them both to another editor in this building. This other editor, you understand, is liable to favor a yarn developed somewhat differently than the ones I favor, even though we may both use stories of the same general character. I am frank to say that I would not have purchased the two stories in any case, even had I been in the other fellow's place. But he did; the fact that I had rejected them made no difference to him."

Mr. Scott added that he has often bought stories rejected by his fellow editors in the Street & Smith organization. His magazine, *Top-Notch*, is one of the veterans of the organization. I should advise any writer who contemplates trying Mr. Scott to make a very careful study of his book before putting paper in the mill. His requirements are closely drawn, as his illuminating articles in THE AUTHOR & JOURNALIST will reveal, and only an analytical perusal of the stories he prints will make clear what they are.

There was just one more editor on my list at this time.

That one was Harold Hersey, of the peppy Clayton publications, which include *Ace-High, Cowboy Stories, The Danger Trail*, the new magazine, *Clues*, added since my visit, and *Ranch Romances*.

Mr. W.M. Clayton, the publisher, started his business several years ago with one lone magazine, *Telling Tales*, now extinct. It was a distinctly different magazine from the usual run at that time, and attracted attention from both readers and authors. I believe it attained a considerable circulation. Then Mr. Clayton and his associates began to branch out, with the result that *Telling Tales* eventually went into the discard. The other magazines of the celebrated Clayton group are of a different, and, in this fast-moving age, more popular type.

I had sold Mr. Hersey several stories in the past. For a time he appeared interested in my work, purchasing promptly at moderate rates. It happens that while I write Western stories, they do not all have cowboys and cowboy activities in them. I turn out quite a number in which I try to portray other picturesque Western characters, such as prospectors, miners, Indians, sheepmen, etc. There are other phases to Western life than cattle raising only, and a demand among readers for stories developed from them.

But Mr. Hersey wants cowboy stories. And as the rates he was paying did not especially attract me I had not written anything strictly for his magazines. Only stories that had been rejected by my regular market went his way. If they happened to be cowboy stories he sometimes bought them; if not, he didn't. And the time came when we ceased doing business.

To tell the truth, I nearly passed up the Hersey visit. It didn't seem worthwhile to bother the gentleman. But as I still had several hours before my train was due to depart, I decided to go.

How glad I am that I did! For as a result of that visit, I have sold Mr. Hersey quite a bunch of stories, at just double the rate he formerly paid me, and have contracted for a series which is already running in *Ace-High*. In fact, to date I have not had a single rejection from him. And all because a half-hour's conversation supplied me with some specific information as to his requirements.

Mr. Hersey was about as different in appearance from what I had pictured him as could be imagined. I had visualized him as a smooth-faced youngster with light-colored hair and a collegiate style of raiment, retiring in disposition and behavior. I gathered the latter impression, I suppose, from the fact that Mr. Hersey's letters are usually very brief and to the point.

I was scarcely prepared, therefore, for the reception that awaited me at the Clayton offices. I had waited in an outer room ten minutes or so when the door flew open, and a muscular gentleman with a shock of dark hair and sleeves rolled almost to his elbows, disclosing hairy forearms, came out.

"Why, hello, Stone," he cried, seizing me by the hand and pumping it so vigorously that he almost jerked my arm out of the socket. "Come into my office. Sit down. When did you get to New York? Ever been here before? How are you, anyway?"

He fairly pushed me into a chair, and settled into his own swivel, regarding me with a broad grin. Hersey is an impressively masculine man, with his heavy shock of gray-streaked hair, his close-clipped mustache, his athletic build, and his vigorous bass voice. The latter fairly booms.

"Perhaps you don't remember me," I began. "But—"

"Remember you!" he cried. "Of course I do. Why, you've sold me—"

And he rattled off the names of the yarns he had purchased from me, faster than I could have done it myself. This, mind you, in spite of the fact that he is now manuscript buyer and editor for three magazines, publishing an average of twenty-seven short stories, a couple of novels, a novelette or two and several serial installments every two weeks out of the year.

"Of course I remember your work," he boomed. "I'd like to be buying it right now, if you'd send me what I want. I lost interest in you because you quit sending me the stuff I required. What was the matter with you?"

I explained that I had sent him only stories previously rejected by my regular market.

"Well, why don't you write something directly for us?" he demanded.

"Because," I said frankly, "I can get more money somewhere else. Your rates have been too low to interest me in original contributions for your magazines."

"How could you expect them to be any higher, when you admit you only offered me seconds?" he retorted. "We can, and do, pay as good rates as almost any all-fiction magazine in the field. But we pay them only to authors who send us the kind of stuff we want."

That interested me.

"For instance, I need a humorous cowboy series right now," he went on. "If you've got anything in mind, let's hear about it."

I outlined, roughly, a humorous cowboy character around whom I had written yarns some years ago, selling them to three different magazines that I recall. Mr. Hersey's eyes snapped.

"That sounds all right to me," he exclaimed. "When you get back home, suppose you do me a story or two and send them in. If I like them I'll buy them, and pay you—"

He named a rate double that he had previously paid me.

"And if they go over all right, I'll do better than that," he added. "Get the first one to me before the end of this month if you can, as I'm going away on a leave of absence about the first. I want to see what it's like." I did so, and he bought promptly He has been buying promptly ever since.

Mr. Hersey has always pursued the policy of discovering and developing authors, encouraging them at every turn and even placing some of them on contract. One popular writer who has been contributing to his books for some years has a contract which calls for four short stories a month and a serial every two months. This man is drawing close to a thousand dollars a month from the Clayton publications alone. Recently he told me that he hasn't had a single rejection for a year and a half!

Mr. Hersey likes authors. His enthusiasm is contagious—and lasting. He knows their problems, and he rejoices in their triumphs. He wants stories of the cow country, for *Ace-High* and *Cowboy Stories*, written in a vein that will interest cowboys as well as readers who never saw the West, and perhaps never will. He likes the rollicking, rough-and-ready, go-get-'em type of yarn, with plenty of humor of the slapstick variety, but authentic nevertheless. Cowboys are traditionally lovers of the practical joke. Hersey likes that kind of humor for his readers. Plenty of gunplay, cattle stampeding, frontier gambling and dancehall festivity, hard riding over the range, roundup work, the galloping of hoofs, the dashing of horns, the bawling of calves, the thick alkali underfoot and in the air—that's the kind of thing this he-man editor wants for his he-man magazines. Fill your stories full of genuine cowboy lingo, if you like. The more the better. Only see that they are *stories!* Let them be filled to bursting with action!

Never bother Hersey with letters unless they're right to the point. He doesn't believe in letters, going or coming, and indulges only in what correspondence he literally has to, professionally speaking. He doesn't believe in rejection slips, either; if he had his way they would never be used.

"If the manuscript comes back, that means that it failed to land," he said. "Why stick a printed slip in with it? If the story merits a letter for any special reason, I believe in writing the letter. But a rejection slip—bah!"

I commend Harold Hersey to writers of Western cowboy stories. He's worth cultivating. But don't waste his time unless you have something worth putting before him. Be sure, first, that your yarn comes somewhere near the bull's-eye represented by the type he is publishing. Then shoot it in, and God bless you! You are apt, very apt indeed, to get one of those classy yellow Clayton checks in return.

[*The Author & Journalist*, January 1927]

Meeting the Editors in Person
General Impressions—The Demand for New Writers "Who Can Deliver the Goods"

"ARE EDITORS WILLING TO HELP authors with suggestions?"

In answer to the above question, propounded in the first of the present series of articles, the writer answered as follows:

"They are, invariably. In fact, they welcome the opportunity to do so."

I based this conclusion upon impressions incidental to a number of personal chats with editors while in New York City several months ago. A query from a reader, however, indicates that some misapprehension may exist regarding the statement. This reader has written in to say that her experience does not bear out mine. Editors have not displayed any eagerness to aid her in any such manner, she declares. When she called one editor's attention to what this writer had said, he replied that he was entirely too busy to criticize the many manuscripts that came to his desk. As this editor happens to be on the staff of *The Saturday Evening Post*, there is no doubt whatever but that he stated the exact situation.

My assertion should have been more comprehensively qualified than it was, of course. Several years ago Robert H. Davis, then managing editor of the Munsey publications, wrote me that a total of forty thousand manuscripts was received by the editors of the Munsey group annually. Other magazine publishing houses today receive even more. It would be a manifest impossibility for these editors to offer many suggestions regarding changes in more than a small proportion of so many stories, no matter how "willing" they might be to do so. Human capacity has a limit.

In last month's issue of THE AUTHOR & JOURNALIST there appeared an article by Arthur E. Scott, editor of *Top-Notch Magazine*. Among other helpful things he said this:

"As the editor of a popular magazine, I get a number of letters and a good many personal calls from would-be authors, and I never have any hesitation in putting before them all the difficulties that lie between a writer and success. *If* they tell me they are not afraid of the work ahead and that they just *have* to write, then I know that possibly I have struck an author in the making, and I am willing to give him all the aid in my power."

Mr. Scott, I think, has set forth the issue clearly. Obviously he cannot give personal attention to every writer who sends in a story for his consideration and asks for suggestions. But after he has become convinced that the writer possesses the talent, command of language, creative ability, imagination, and staying qualities essential to progress in authorship—ah! That is a different story. Now he is not only "willing" to help the aspiring one with helpful suggestions, but he makes it perfectly clear that he welcomes the opportunity to do so.

In other words, a process of elimination must perforce be resorted to. There are of course, thousands of persons bombarding the magazines with material who have few, if any, qualifications for successful authorship. Their literary efforts show this lack. Some of our most highly educated persons fail utterly when they attempt to write fiction. As Mr. Scott points out, they may lack imagination, creative ability and the capacity for employing language convincingly. The most helpful suggestion they could receive, perhaps, would be to cease their efforts in this direction.

Each year a new crop of promising young authors appears. You may be sure that they are "the survival of the fittest." They have started side by side with hundreds, and perhaps thousands, of others who have thus far failed to sell any of their product. It is these promising, persistent, talented few who get the helpful suggestions from the editors. The others have not yet fought their way far enough out of the ruck to engage special editorial attention.

With a single exception, all the editors I talked with in New York specified the necessity of careful study of their respective magazines as an essential to successful disposal of manuscripts to them.

Authors who meet this requirement, they told me, are the ones who receive the earliest editorial attention and help. If a story received comes within the exactions of the magazine's policies, is neatly typed and spaced, and adequately margined, employs the particular style of capitalization required, bears evidences of having been carefully conceived, does not violate the modern standards of literary ethics, is compactly built, and so on—why shouldn't the editor be favorably impressed? As a matter of fact, he is likely to be immensely flattered. The chances are fifty to one that he will pause in the grind of his duties to dictate a letter to the author—if he does not actually buy the yarn—and offer some of the "helpful suggestions" we are talking about. He will have discovered an author in the making, as Mr. Scott cites, and will be anxious to help develop that promising tyro.

The competition among writers in the fields of fiction is exceptionally keen. But be of good cheer—you will forge ahead in the race if you have the necessary qualifications and give your chosen profession the same amount of energy and study that you would give to any other. Let me particularly emphasize the word *study*. That means something more than just writing your own special brand of fiction and trying to induce an editor to buy it. A law student would never gain admittance to the bar by any such method.

Years ago, before I had sold my first story, Matthew White, Jr., rejected one of my hopeful offerings with the following comment:

"Two things I like about this story are its Western atmosphere, and its brevity—two thousand five hundred words. . . . If these hints are of any value to you, try us again."

While I was talking to a certain well-known editor, on the occasion of my New York visit, reference was made to the work of a prolific writer. He is one of the "fiction foundries" of the profession, turning out many hundreds of thousands of words annually. This editor, it appeared, cares only moderately for the author's work, notwithstanding which he buys quite a bit of it every year.

"The reason?" he repeated. "Why, he submits a lot of stories so short that they are valuable to me as fillers. One of the hardest jobs an editor has, according to my experience, is to find really short stories."

The cardinal failing of the average short story writer is prolixity, this editor declared. "Ropey" yarns are the rule rather than the exception. Short stories are always in more demand than serials, novels or novelettes, but *long* short-stories, running to awkward lengths between 6000 and 15,000 words, have the smallest chance of sale unless they are exceptionally strong as to plot and compactness. There are authors, to be sure, who succeed in selling this type of story with flattering regularity; but they sell in *spite* of their unsuitability as to length, rather than because of the latter.

"More *short* short-stories; that's what we want!" cry the editors.

I know a young author who received three cents a word for his first, sale, from an all-fiction magazine editor. I congratulated him, not without considerable envy. A few months later another writing acquaintance, in the same city, sold *his* first story to another all-fiction magazine—and he, too, received three cents a word.

In each case the check was for $75, and the story was 2500 words in length. Not long afterward a third literary friend sold a story to the first-cited magazine. It was one of the longer variety. The check was a fairly generous one; but when he computed it on a word-rate basis, he found that he had received only a trifle more than one cent a word.

Still another friend of mine sold a story to a widely-circulated magazine, receiving about a cent and a half a word. Encouraged by his success—he was at the time a neophyte at the game—he submitted a second yarn, this time about twice as long as the first one. To his consternation his check was *less* than the one sent him for the first, and shorter, story! He wrote a protesting inquiry. The editor replied:

"Your second story was really longer than we usually care to print in our magazine. Therefore it is worth less to us than the shorter one. That is why your second check was smaller than the first."

The moral to all this is, obviously: "Hold your stories down in length." Even if they have less of actual merit, your chances of sale are relatively greater. If your story idea has real merit, on the other hand, and you are able to judge it fairly as such, you will be reasonably safe in using as many words in the telling as seem necessary to adequate portrayal.

There seems to be a lot of misunderstanding as to the proper classification of certain magazines sometimes designated as "highbrow," when perhaps they should be known merely as "high class," or "higher class."

I refer to such publications as *The Saturday Evening Post*, *Hearst's International*, *The American*, *Pictorial Review*, *The Red Book*, etc., as distinguished from *The Century*, *Atlantic Monthly*, *Harper's*, *The American Mercury*, and *Scribner's*.

The last-named five are distinctly "highbrow." They have a high literary standard, and cater only to the most discriminating readers. Their circulations doubtless do not compare, in quantity, with those of the first-named group. And the experience of writers of my acquaintance who have sold them material indicates that very high rates cannot be expected, although their rates as a rule go considerably beyond those paid by the all-fiction magazines.

The first-named group may be considered as "higher-class" than the wood-pulp magazines. Not long ago a certain popular writer of my acquaintance gleefully showed me a letter from one of them, offering him a thousand dollars for a short story of about 7500 words. Such rates are out of the question from any but magazines of immense circulations and heavy advertising patronage. They are perhaps "higher-class," but they can hardly be called "highbrow." Sales of fiction to these publications are apt to be few and far between.

It seems to me that personal contact with editors does much to stimulate story-writing effort. I have been increasingly conscious of this since the New York visit. I brought away some very pleasant impressions, and I frequently find myself taking greater pains with a story than I used to do, because I have in mind the personality of the editor to whom I am about to submit it.

I think I realize, as never before, the exacting requirements with which the average editor is hedged about. These range from reader-demands to business-office limitations. When he buys a story from a new author he is taking a risk, betting his story-judgment against the probable reception of the yarn by the readers. He may lose his bet; sometimes, indeed, he does. His value in his position lies in his ability to select and print winners.

This means, of, course, that a writer should look beyond his own selfish interests when he writes and submits a story to an editor. He should bear in mind that the editor's job is to produce a magazine for which people will pay their money, and not rue their outlay of time and cash. He cannot produce such a magazine with shoddy material; and he cannot get first-class material unless writers produce it. Therefore the writer and the editor are indispensable to each other. The nearer the writer comes to producing salable material, the more the editor will come to depend upon him.

I am thoroughly convinced that the conviction of so many aspiring authors that the unknown writer "has no chance" is utterly without foundation. Scarcely a month goes by that a new magazine is not launched. A fair proportion of them survive. Where there was one magazine published in New York a few years ago there are forty today. Many millions of words are purchased by these magazines every month. The so-called "unknown" author is more eagerly welcomed now than ever before.

In my own experience, I recall that a fellow writer, who is now a national literary celebrity, once offered to aid me by recommending me to an editor to whom I had sold several stories. A little later, sure enough, I received a letter from this editor, telling me that my author-friend had dropped into his office and told him of knowing me personally.

"He says you're all right," the letter said. "Bully for you; I'll help you all I can." And then he proceeded to reject my stories with such speed and precision that I almost decided to quit trying. It took me a long time to live down that well-meant recommendation, and to get back on my feet. I really believe that after the "boost" that editor scrutinized my offerings with a jaundiced eye. Certainly he established a record for steady and uninterrupted rejections from then on.

I know of one case in which an author, who has been producing salable work for years, refuses to have any personal relations with an editor to whom he has sold a great deal of stuff. The author, as I understand it, once took offense at what he branded as "careless" the handling of a situation in one of his stories, and protested so violently that the editor, who is as human as anybody else, retaliated in kind. The mistake had not been his fault, but the author insisted that it had been. The "tiff" wound up as many others have, before and since. The two don't speak to each other unless if is absolutely necessary.

But does this strained personal relation make any difference in their professional dealings? It does not. The editor buys the author's contributions as regularly as before, and is glad to get them. When he reads one of the author's offerings he does so without prejudice. The reason is simple.

"I'm here to turn out the best magazine I am capable of getting together," he explains. "This author turns out the kind of stories my readers like. He helps me to produce a salable book. It is my job to buy his stories, and print them, regardless of my personal feelings. I can't afford to take any other attitude."

Since my return home the conviction has grown upon me that fiction-writers, upon however small a scale, are performing a very definite service in contributing to the great program of clean, legitimate entertainment of millions of people in America. One senses this when he views the mammoth scale upon which magazines and books are manufactured in New York.

Recently a helper on the ice wagon which supplies my home paused to tell me something just after he had replenished the ice box. He is a little fellow, well past middle age, and slightly crippled. He does not look like a man who has had an overabundance of the good things of life. I am quite sure that he has no surplus to spend on automobiles, radios or picture shows.

"I read one of your stories in the —— magazine last night," he informed me. "I read that magazine right along. Thought you might like to know."

He left me with more of a glow in my heart than he could possibly guess. He can buy the magazine in question for fifteen cents, and it will supply him with reading entertainment for several nights out of the week. I find myself feeling grateful that I am privileged to have an humble part in providing it for him!

[*The Author & Journalist*, January 1928]

Damning the Editor
Arthur E. Scott

[Notes on Scott's career accompany his *Meeting the Editors in Person* profile. :: In reading the below, one experiences a proverbial dash of cold water upon realizing that the anticipated damnation will not be forthcoming. But the disappointment is quickly replaced by the small mystery contained in Scott's shoptalk yarn—the identity of Scott's anonymous author-friend—whose solution we leave as an exercise for the reader. :: In the last section here, Scott does a nice job of rebutting the "speed writing theory" quoted with his career notes.]

ONE OF THE MOST POPULAR AMUSEMENTS of writers who get a considerable part of their work returned as unavailable is that of damning the editor. "The editor is no good; he is inconsiderate; probably he never read the manuscript; he has no use for newcomers"; and so forth ad infinitum. On the other hand, the writer who finds a quick market for his material, and gets far more checks than rejections, thinks the editors are pretty good fellows, who know their jobs and appreciate good work no matter from whom it may come. If these very conflicting opinions were submitted to any competent judge there would be no doubt as to the verdict he would render.

Arthur E. Scott

Damning the editor is poor sport. In the vast majority of cases it is not fair; there is no justification for it. Further, it betrays a streak in the writer's character that should be remedied if he is to get on in his profession. The editor's judgment of a manuscript is, in at least ninety-nine cases out of a hundred, much better than the author's. Naturally the editor knows what is best suited for his magazine; the author is a poor judge of that, and the manuscript may not have been written with any particular magazine in view.

Mind, I am not claiming any degree of infallibility for editors. They do make mistakes, like everyone else, authors not excepted. But if they do, they are honest mistakes, at which no one should complain. And if one editor makes a mistake and rejects a good story, another editor will be found who will send a check for it.

There is a considerable difference between damning an editor and criticizing his decision. An author may take it upon himself to criticize a rejection—though I may say it is seldom either wise or worth while—and the editor may go to the trouble of pointing out just why the manuscript in question is not suitable for his magazine.

Two or three years ago a letter, anonymous, appeared in *The Authors' League Bulletin* in which the writer assailed editors in general, saying that they did not want an author's best work once he had got a reputation for blood-and-thunder stuff, which the readers enjoyed. The writer stated that he had spent a long time on a story and polished it up until it was far above his usual standard, and the editor to whom he sent it returned it with a note that he did not want that kind of material from him. Therefore, the writer concluded, there is no use in an author's trying to turn out really literary work, when the slapdash stuff is more appreciated.

I could not let this letter pass unchallenged. I replied in a later issue of the *Bulletin*, signing myself a popular-fiction magazine editor. As the writer of the first letter concealed his identity, I did likewise.

I wrote that everything the writer had said was absurd; in ten or more years of editorial work I had never heard of an editor's refusing a man's work because it was too well done. I told him that when one of my writers did better work than he had been in the habit of turning out, I raised his rate. I told him that the stuff which he dashed off and sold had undoubtedly some attractiveness about it which appealed to the readers, and that when he began to revise and polish up his work, in all probability he polished it until whatever original charm it possessed was gone, rubbed out. What I got for my trouble was the remark contained in a short letter from the original writer in the next *Bulletin* to the effect that any man who had spent over ten years as a popular-fiction magazine editor had lost all sense of literary values.

Some time later I met a well-known writer, and we became good friends. From several remarks which he made I came to the conclusion that my new friend was my hitherto unknown antagonist in the *Bulletin*, and I said so. He did not admit the fact, so that to this day I have no knowledge as to whether I was right or not. But a curious development followed.

My friend happened to mention that he had one manuscript which he could not sell, that several editors had turned it down on account of its length, which was, he said, twenty thousand words. I replied that such a length was no objection to me, and I asked him to send me the story.

He did, and I read the tale with great expectations. My friend told me he considered this was his best work, and that he had spent a month in the locality of which he wrote in order to get the color correctly done. Naturally I was delighted to get the story that represented this author's best work, as I had never had anything submitted by him before, and I looked forward to featuring it on the cover. Alas, for my hopes! The manuscript was a beautifully written piece of work, polished to the *nth* degree, and the descriptive matter could hardly be excelled. It was a wonderful word picture of the place and its people; but of story it had none!

Sadly I gave it back to my friend and told him what I thought about it. He asked me if I considered he should rewrite it. My answer was that he should get a story first.

There is little doubt that the other editors who returned this manuscript saying that the length rendered it unavailable were not being perfectly frank with the author. I was absolutely frank, and I think he appreciated it. Anyway, we are still friends.

It seems perfectly plain to me that this twenty-thousand-word story was the one on which my friend had labored so long and which was continually rejected by the editors. He had endeavored to do a piece of fine writing, and had succeeded in his object; but he, who is noted for his stirring tales of plot and action, either forgot to get them into this story or later polished them out.

There is in the minds of many writers a conflict between popular fiction and literary work which should not exist. I admit at once that the bulk of popular fiction can hardly by any stretch of the imagination be called literary; there is a reason why this is so, although there is no reason why it must be so. The reason why it is so is because popular fiction is turned out rapidly, in quantity, to sell quickly, and work deserving of the term "literary" cannot be written in such fashion. There is no reason, however, beyond a financial one, why popular fiction should not be written in a highly polished literary style; if a good story was there, no reader would object to the fine manner in which it was written.

I have published a football story that was as fine a bit of popular fiction as I want to read, and not until after the story was printed did it occur to me that the story had no plot. The picture drawn was so fascinating that it held the reader's attention just as closely as a striking mystery.

I published another football story by the same author that gave me a choking feeling in the throat; as fine a piece of writing as I have seen, and a story I shall never forget. I thought I had a "find" in this author, who lives by writing stories of sport, but he told me to my great regret that it took him five or six months to turn out stories like those. The stories he lived by were of a different caliber, and he found no fault with me for rejecting them.

That is the mark of the professional writer. He offers you his wares for sale; if they are what you want, you buy them; if they are not what you want, you decline them with thanks. The professional writer does not damn the editor because he does not accept his offerings, any more than a shoe salesman would damn a customer who leaves his store without making a purchase because the salesman does not carry the exact style of shoe the customer wants.

The editor is always just as anxious to buy as you are to sell, but he is going to buy goods suitable for his use, and the chances are in favor of his being the best judge of what he can use to advantage.

[*Writer's Digest*, March 1928]

The Enterprising Author
Emil Zubryn

[Frank Engs Blackwell (~1878-1951), the subject of this interview, reported for the *New York Herald* as a young man. He was a feature writer for the *New York Sun* when he applied for a position at Street & Smith editing dime novels. Blackwell got the job by doing a great rewrite on a shoddily-written Frank Merriwell novel. Later, S&S created the first specialized detective pulp, *Detective Story Magazine* (first issue, October 5, 1915), with Blackwell as editor. He performed a similar duty for *Western Story* in 1919, added *Far West* in 1926 and *Best Detective* in 1929. Blackwell was described in the May 1922 *The Student Writer* thusly: "He has a pear-shaped head, almost bald, and isn't sensitive about it. He dignifies a derby, and if destiny hadn't designed him for an editor, he might have been a detective. This is the feeling he gives, but, outside of delving into detective and Western yarns, he is chiefly interested in horses." In the '20s, Blackwell rose to the position of Managing Editor. In 1930, he was point man in the development of another pioneering title, *The Shadow*, including the hiring of Walter Gibson to write the novels. In late '37, S&S underwent a major shakeup, with many titles canceled and Blackwell promoted to Editor-in-Chief. It appears, though, that he left the company in the middle of '38. How he spent his remaining years is unclear, though he did surface with a short story in the January 1945 *Detective Story*. :: Little could be discovered about Emil Zubryn. In 1946, he started a magazine called *The Free Lance Weekly*, a bulletin devoted to freelancers of all stripes. In 1949, he had a radio script produced for the *Radio City Playhouse*.]

WE CALLED ON MR. F.E. BLACKWELL in his editorial sanctum in the Street & Smith Building, on Seventh Avenue, an imposing red brick structure that houses the various periodicals that are published by this concern. After a few preliminary greetings Mr. Blackwell began his discourse on the writer and the writing profession.

By means of cited examples he proved that whereas a lawyer who resides in the country or a doctor in a small town may gain some name for themselves in their own locality, in another city they are unknown.

"But consider the writer and you have a marked difference," continued Mr. Blackwell. "He may live in a garret in Greenwich Village or in the tenement district. He may be north, south, east or west, in a small town or in a large city, it does not matter. The writer sells a story to a magazine and it is published, it attracts the attention of the readers and they clamor for more. In time, the writer becomes world famous. He is known the world over and his name is immediately recognized by a vast majority of readers."

Mr. Blackwell dwelt on the fact that many of his contributors are scattered all over the world and we had the pleasure of reading several post cards and letters from contributors in France, Germany and other countries. Very few of his writers have met Mr. Blackwell personally, but they all correspond and send their compliments to him from time to time.

"Another important point that I desire to bring out to the enterprising author," he said, "is: Are you really interested in writing or merely intrigued by the life that an author leads?"

Mr. Blackwell smiled as he recalled an incident during his boyhood. It seems that he spent one summer in the Adirondacks and while there he had noticed several artists painting landscapes. He secretly worshipped them and decided that he would become an artist. Returning home he invested in crayons and tried his hand at drawing but soon tired of it. He did not want to draw but to lead the life of an artist, a care free and easy going sort of existence.

"—and it is the same with many young men and women," averred the editor. "They come to see me. They are attracted by the glamour of the writing profession but there is one chief fault with them all—they can not write because of lack of training. Just as a lawyer and a doctor serve an apprenticeship, so, too, must the young writer.

"Eventually many of the beginners tire of writing and receiving nothing but rejection slips for their pains and they go back to the office and the shop, back to the tasks for which they are fitted. It is best that they do so for otherwise they would only waste much of their valuable time."

The talking turned to personal matters and then we began inquiring about the needs of the Street & Smith people, particularly those magazines that are edited by Mr. Blackwell.

Mr. Blackwell has served as an editor for that firm approximately sixteen years and during those years has been responsible for the discovery of many new writers. As for the editorial needs and the treatment of manuscripts while at his office we will let Mr. Blackwell explain:

"The Street & Smith Company purchase a tremendous number of manuscripts each year. *Western Story, Detective Story,* and *Far West Illustrated* alone take some 9,000,000 words of manuscript per year. This is a tremendous amount for several magazines but it only proves that here is a market for the writer who really can write.

"We are, of course, always willing to examine manuscripts that are suitable for our publications. *The Far West Illustrated Magazine* is, as its name implies, an all western fiction magazine. The stories should deal with life in the open and may include Canada, Alaska, and Mexico, as well as the West.

"The short stories should be from 2000 to 8000 words in length and have action in every page. We are also in the market for novels and novelettes of appropriate length.

"The needs of *Western Story Magazine* are practically the same as for *The Far West Illustrated*.

"Then there is *Detective Story Magazine*. For this publication unusual detective stories, mystery stories, and stories dealing with crime are favored.

"We also use some verse for the western magazines and articles that express some idea that is not hackneyed."

The Street & Smith Group is one of the oldest established fiction magazine groups and it would well repay the writer to cultivate this market. A study of the various magazines will give one a general idea of the requirements and then, if the author desires an acceptance slip, he had better write a story that is as good as and even better than those that have been published.

A manuscript is bound to get a pretty fair reading at the Street & Smith office and it is considered very carefully. If rejected there is a very good reason for the rejection.

Often enough when Mr. Blackwell comes upon a promising writer he takes the time and trouble to write a note of criticism. In this way he has helped quite a few writers. He is a cheery individual and not at all like the hard hearted editor that he is supposed to represent.

The rate of payment is one that is well worth the time of writers. If we remember correctly it ranks from 1-½ cent a word and up.

In closing this article we would like to end with the parting words of Mr. Blackwell: "The dictionary is your lumber yard. It is for you, the writer, to study the words and so put them together that they make sense and interesting reading."

[*The Author & Journalist*, November 1928]

An Experiment in Cooperation
Harold Hersey

[The idea Hersey presents here sounds good on paper, but the coming Depression made the higher word-rates unsustainable.]

WHEN I RESIGNED AS SUPERVISING EDITOR of the Macfadden Publications two days before last Christmas, I was the proud possessor of around $500 and a lot of dreams—with perhaps more hope than faith.

Now that I am editing magazines of my new string of publications, a review of the past eight months might be of interest to the readers of THE AUTHOR & JOURNALIST.

I went up to my mother's place in Highland, New York, with the idea that I was going to quit the editorial game for some time to come. Ten days after reaching there, I launched a magazine known as *Swap*. All that I can say about this periodical is that it was the third failure out of twenty-one years of successes. Of course, my enemy friends and my friendly enemies can look at the failure and forget *Ace-High*, *The Quill*, *Cowboy Stories*, *Clues*, *The Ledernier Cri*, and others, since I started editing and mis-editing. Here in New York there is always much more excitement about a failure than there is about a success. I suppose that many people were as much surprised as I was when I promptly paid for all the literary material in the second issues of my new string and established this new company as a practical entity in the publishing field.

I stayed up in Highland until I joined *Elite Styles Magazine* with a share in the profits. I came to New York and got out one issue before financial troubles developed around this whole magazine, and learning that there was little hope at that time of climbing over the wall of indebtedness, I joined The Eastern Distributing Corporation as general editorial advisor. I had had numerous offers from various publishing houses but my one idea during this hit-or-miss period was not to slip into mere harness again. I wanted something in which I had a stake and a full opportunity to make returns on my time, my experience, and whatever knowledge life had given me. Therefore, when Mr. John F. Edwards and myself carried into being the new Magazine Publishers Incorporated, I was happy once more. Here was a chance to fulfill the dream of many months—to issue a string of pulp-paper magazines similar to those I handled at various periods during the past.

Thus was born the Hersey Group: *Western Trails*, *Flying Aces*, *The Dragnet*, and *Under Fire*. And soon after launching these four, we absorbed *Golden West* and *Underworld*—two periodicals that had only been using reprint material. However, beginning with their December issues in my hands they will use only new stuff. Now I am adding two more, another flying magazine and a film magazine, names to be announced later.

As I look back over these months I realize that it is a good thing for a man who has held a job all his life to ride the rails ever so often. Especially is this good for an editor. It teaches him to understand other angles of the publishing business. In this particular instance, it gave me a realization of the difficulties that surround any venture of this sort. After all, a magazine is like a play. The big difference is that a monthly magazine has thirty first nights instead of one. And if it succeeds then it becomes a stock vaudeville company with a new variety each issue. In my own case, it is purely a stock company because those writers who start with me remain with me. Why should I, if a magazine succeeds, go over the head of the public and buy from new authors if my old ones continue to send me excellent material? This was my policy while senior editor of the Clayton Magazines and it will continue to be my policy while handling these periodicals.

The editorial ideal behind these magazines is a simple one: *Entertain the reader.* The successful writer is a natural-born storyteller. He is a recurring phenomenon like the Minnesingers of the Middle Ages, but instead of going from castle to castle he goes from person to person through the medium of the printed page. What is the difference, my Masters? To hold this audience, if he were talking to them personally, he would first of all have to entertain them.

I beg my writers and my prospective writers to tell their stories simply. Characterization and local color play just as important parts as plot.

Each of my magazines is edited individually. I do not like pseudo-scientific stuff: trips to the moon in aeroplanes. I do not like straight adventure yarns for the simple reason that the public doesn't want to read them in large quantities. I do not like stories with mushy girl interest. I do not like stories where the writer parades knowledge that he has just gained from reading the encyclopedia, and I become quite irritated over the Western writer who lives in China and has seen the wild and woolly only in the movies. The same holds true with the aviation writer, detective writer, and the war writer.

Now comes the important part of my announcement. My rate of payment will be determined as follows:

Per Word	*No. of Sales for Each Magazine*
1 cent	50,000
1½ cents	50,000 – 75,000
2 cents	75,000 – 100,000
2½ cents	100,000 – 125,000
3 cents	125,000 – 150,000

There is no use going any higher until the time comes. If the occasion arises, you can rest assured that I will go as far as my circulation allows without losing my courage. Average sales over a four or six-month period will be used as a basis for determining the rates.

The above is predicated on an idea of cooperation in the publishing business that I have had in the back of my head for many moons. In other words, why shouldn't the author bear some of the brunt that goes with the success or failure of a given periodical? I have only my record to stand on when it comes to fulfilling promises to those authors who have chosen to join me in the early days and who have stood with me during the later days of success. This is my answer to the undoubted questions that will follow the above: How about the writer who joins now? And what will happen to him if or when one of my magazines goes over?

Harold Hersey

Lastly, I want to say that at this writing payments have just been completed on the second issues, which means that we are handling the financial side of this business on a thirty to sixty day basis. In the future, stories purchased will be paid for when the issues containing them come from the press. I have decided to consider each periodical on its individual merits. Circulation figures and payments will be determined purely with the rise or fall of the individual magazine and the individual writer. We are not putting out canned soup. Each magazine is an entity, a living thing, and it stands or falls upon its component parts. And for this reason the writer can afford to give his best, knowing that he will profit by his investment if he does so.

[*Writers' Markets and Methods*, June 1929]

A Letter From Arthur J. Burks

[The prolific Arthur J. Burks (1898-1974) was prolific in every field that attracted him: adventure, aviation, boxing, detective, horror, science fiction, and weird menace. About the only fields he steered clear of were romance and western. Also, with few exceptions, he avoided series characters which precluded him from ever writing a hero title. The million-words-a-year man had the energy but not the attention span. He began writing in 1920 but struggled to make serious sales. In 1923, he enrolled in a correspondence course from The Palmer Institute of Authorship (formerly The Palmer Photoplay Corporation) in Hollywood, while still a Second Lieutenant in the Marines, and learned to polish his technique. A photoplay course with the school never bore fruit—outside of a play produced in Los Angeles—but the pulp career really took off with a strong record of sales from 1925 forward. As one of Palmer's prize graduates, he submitted many letters and articles to the school magazine, *Writers' Markets and Methods*, including the below, addressed to Palmer's chief, William David Ball. In the letter, he meets with Clayton editor Allan K. Echols about stories intended for *Air Adventures*. The stories did indeed find their way into the magazine, but only after it had changed its name to *Flyers*: "Wings of Ebony" (November 1929) and "Wings of Chaos" (March 1930).]

Dear Bill:

Well, since I haven't anything really important to do, I'll drop you a line or two. Besides, I've got something to say. To begin with, I only dragged one thousand berries out of the grab-pile for April, mostly because I been so busy dodging streetcars in the big city, and looking breathlessly up at the tall buildings. Howsoever, I've a hunch May will be fairer and warmer.

But lemme begin at the beginning. I arrived in New York City, where I immediately went into executive session with the barber and got myself more or less presentable, when I hied myself to Fiction House, since which time I have been hie-ing myself not only to Fiction House but to other houses as well, and so far I haven't grabbed a rejection since my arrival here. So I guess it pays to blow your own horn in person.

Well, anyway, Jack Kelly, Treasurer of Fiction House, allowed as how, in view of all the deathless stuff I've sold 'em in the last year or so, that I should be led forth to one of the exclusive clubs and properly dined (note that I didn't say *wined* and dined), or rather luncheoned, and he gave me a rather unique experience in that he took his reading and editorial staff along with him.

I wondered why he put me at the head of the table, but there was method in Jack's madness. Here before me were all the readers who had been rejecting, accepting, and usually cussing me out, over a period of years, together with editors who cussed over my stuff when they had to change the rhyme and meter thereon.

Jack Kelly started the ball rolling by introducing all those paid slaves to the visiting genius—me—and after we had seated ourselves, he spoke right out in meeting, explaining why I had been seated at the head of the table, with a round dozen of men of various and assorted sizes and complexions, to right and left of me.

"Well," says Jack, "here is the jury, and here is the accused! What could be sweeter? Freeman (one of the editors), you've frequently said that Burks was a rotten writer and that if you had your way he'd still be doing squads east in the Marines. Suppose you tell him to his face exactly what you think about it?"

Jack wasn't funning, especially, and Freeman, who was himself an old-timer in the Marines while I was screaming for a bottle or because a pin was sticking me, began to question me anent my Marine Corps experience . . . and before he got through he asked me why I had never written the story of the "Heroes of Samar." Everybody leaned forward to listen to our gabbing about it, since we both knew most of the stories concerning that terrible experience in Samar of Uncle Sam's Marines, and when we called a halt, Jack Kelly snapped at me:

"Write it! It's a natural!"

I did. The title is "Swords of Samar," and I got four hundred fish for it . . . all because Freeman had started asking questions to test me. I thanked Freeman very courteously, and he got the job of writing a 3000-word blurb for the story. Then Bob Carter, who edits *Air Stories*, *Aces* and *Wings*, asked me why the heck I didn't do a serial laid in a city, dealing with aviation of tomorrow. I did that, too; but it didn't get in in time to make my report for April as big as May's report should be if I don't stub my toe or something. So, a novelette and a serial grew out of a luncheon given me by Fiction House, in which the "jury gazed upon the prisoner, and the prisoner gazed upon the jury."

Then a most peculiar thing happened. A friend of mine was here in New York, and since I was on the way myself, I asked him to go to Allan K. Echols, and ask him about a story entitled "Wings of Ebony," and see could he maybe get a check to hold for my arrival. He wired me, out there in the wilds of Los AngHellees: " 'Wings of Ebony' rejected, because of which no check will be waiting therefore. Where do I send the corpse?"

It appeared, then, that "Wings of Ebony" had been sent back, and hadn't reached Los AngHellees before I left. So, I hadn't left a forwarding address because I didn't know where I was going to, and didn't want bill collectors getting wise anyway, and the bulky manuscript, with a return address of the publisher in the left-hand corner, went back to the publisher, who innocently opened it up, thought it had been submitted again, probably cussed because there was no return envelope—*and bought the story!* Another four hundred mackerel!

I just this minute had lunch with Echols, of *Air Adventures*, one of the Clayton group, and told him about this. He denied it all very vigorously, and simply explained that he had made a mistake in titles when he had told my friend "Wings of Ebony" had been returned; but it *does* make a good story, doesn't it, so I'm always going to tell it that way. And while I'm speaking of Al Echols, I'd like to tell you something he told me today, and which he gave me permission to repeat.

It had to do with manuscripts which came into his office, and is of value to every writer who is trying to make the grade. "You know," he said, "that if every writer could look at the slush (which Echols called all submitted material by people whose names were not known to the force) that comes in here, and see how we handle it, I've got a hunch a lot more of them would see the value of preparation. For instance, I never read a pencil or pen-and-ink manuscript. The story might be good—we've got some of our finest stories out of the 'slush,' written in many instances *by people who were never able to sell us anything afterward*—but I have to read a lot of stuff, and can't take a chance on ruining my eyes by reading a long yarn of which the writer thought too little to have typewritten. If he thought too little of it to typewrite it, or have it done, why should *I* think a lot of it . . . and if he doesn't know any better, he probably doesn't know how to write stories! Then I notice preparation, whether the writer knows his stuff or not. If there are no indentations for paragraphs, he doesn't. The story may be good, mind, but it's too much work to edit it, and besides, that's what we pay the writer for doing. I can usually tell whether a story clicks with me or not within the first five hundred words. In that length a story either flops or goes over. . . ."

Here I interrupted Mr. Echols to tell him that a story of mine he had rejected, sending along a letter to the effect that he had only read the first page or two and that the yarn didn't seem to go anywhere, had been purchased by another organization at a price extremely pleasing to me.

"I don't give a cuss," says he, "it wasn't *our* beginning, and it's our beginnings I'm interested in!"

"How does a poor writer tell?" I queried.

"You know darned well how!" he retorted. "What you doing? Interviewing me for some writers' magazine? How does a writer tell, indeed! He studies our magazines to find out what we want . . . and then most of 'em give us something different!"

I might interpolate that it was just because I had given Mr. Echols a story that was vastly different from anything I had hitherto sent him, that he had asked me to lunch to talk it over! From which one would gather that the whole thing is more or less hit or miss. It isn't. Echols explained it: "Your story is different, yes; but it came in exactly at the time we were looking for exactly that kind of yarn. It wouldn't happen again in a hundred years, and you're really lucky to have met me, don't you know? We were planning to run a 'different' novel occasionally, and had just sold ourselves on the idea, and were wondering where to get these here different novels, when in trips 'Wings of Chaos,' your story, to answer our prayer. We haven't bought it, yet, mind you, or I wouldn't be spending ninety cents to give you a lunch and have a talk-fest, but we're planning . . ."

And then he told me about a new venture I'm not at liberty to discuss at the moment, but which I'll give you the dope on when I get permission to speak.

Yes, I've also had an experience with a fly-by-night publisher, for whom I hope none of you chaps and chapettes have written; but there are libel laws, and so I'll just slip the name to you, Bill, and you can whisper it to the boys and girls who care to ask. This magazine publisher took a 20,000-word story which I had had around for a year or so, and promised payment on a certain date. It hasn't been made yet, though I've done everything but call out the Marines; nor will the editor return the manuscript without a legal battle, though why he likes it so well, I can't see. At least a dozen other editors didn't like it at all! But even if it *was* old stuff, and maybe looked it, he didn't have to take it, and he shouldn't have promised to pay and then sent only his apologies. If I weren't here on the ground I might lose this money; but I'm here, and I'm a darned sight bigger than he is, and he may push me too far yet!

Now Bill, don't worry about me. I haven't got run over yet, and will probably survive and get back to Hollywood when the roses bloom again, and I have made all the personal contacts I think I may need in my business.

I just have one real trouble here. I've had four secretaries to date, and am still trying to get one to suit me. Those who can type off good copy are homely as old maid sin, and the swell looking ones can't spell!

Hoping you are the same, I am,
Arthur J. Burks.

[*The Author & Journalist*, July 1929]

Editors You Want To Know: W. Adolphe Roberts
Frances Dublin

[*Editors You Want To Know* was a regular feature which petered out in 1930. Most of the profiles were of pulp editors, all of which are included here. :: Walter Adolphe Roberts (1886-1962) was born in Kingston, Jamaica. He left home for the wide world at age 18. Our earliest known publication for him is a poem in the July 1906 *Munsey's* as Walter Adolf Roberts. He belonged to Greenwich Village's literary renaissance in the prewar years, associating with Margaret Sanger and Edna St. Vincent Millay. He appeared in the pulps as early as 1915, with a short in *All-Story*. During the war, he worked in *The Brooklyn Eagle's* Paris bureau with famed commentator H.V. Kaltenborn. After returning to America, he edited *Ainslee's*, which he conceded was a "trashy" magazine. He published a book of poetry in 1919. After *Ainslee's*, Roberts was an associate editor of *Hearst's International* under Ray Long. He appeared in a number of magazines through the late-teens and '20s including *Pearson's*, *The Smart Set*, *Everybody's*, *Argosy*, and *Breezy Stories*. His "as told to" byline started appearing in *Ghost Stories* with its second issue (August 1926). Roberts took the editorial reins of *Ghost Stories* for the first half of 1928, then moved on to *Brief Stories*, leaving the magazine after nine months when it was sold from Harper & Brothers to the McKinnon-Fly Company. His magazine work disappears after 1930 as he dedicated himself to his books, becoming a prolific author of travel books and historical novels, many of them centered around the Caribbean. In the '30s, he became a leader of a Jamaican independence movement which finally realized its goal mere months before his death. At some point, Roberts became classified as an African-American writer, which would have made him the first black author of a mystery novel (*The Haunting Hand*, 1926). But he disputed the classification, writing a prominent bookseller of African-American literature in 1954: "Please be advised that I am not a Negro, or of Negro ancestry. Will you please remove my name from your list."]

WHEN W. ADOLPHE ROBERTS WAS CALLED in last October to edit *Brief Stories*, he had already made a name for himself as editor of a wide range of magazines. It was no great surprise, then, to the public that this magazine should quickly take on a new and more vital character under the expert guidance of the present editor. Readers have warmly responded to the policy of a varied table of contents, ranging from stirring adventures, virile fighting stories, to tales of romantic love. The ideal of a modern short-story magazine, in other words, is fast taking shape; and *Brief Stories* bids fair to become one of the most popular fiction periodicals.

Which merely confirms the judgment of those who are familiar with Mr. Roberts' career. A man of sound literary perception, he brings to his job the fruit of many years' wide experience; not only in the immediate task of editing magazines, but in other ways—as himself a writer of distinction; war correspondent, author of mystery stories and serous novels; and highest of all, poet of some of the truest verse that has come out of the United States.

But if his achievements seem especially to fit him to his present task, his experiences, in a wider sense, have equally contributed to his success. His life itself has been filled with adventures; hence, that sense which can detect the note of adventure in stories has been quickened and made keener by the many he himself has known.

W. Adolphe Roberts

Elsewhere, he has told how as a mere youth of sixteen, he broke loose from all family ties to go in search of adventure in strange places and climes, finally landing a job as a reporter in Kingston, Jamaica. After a year of journalism in the tropics, he journeyed on to San Francisco, where he worked on the *Chronicle* and sold his first short-stories to Bret Harte's old magazine, *The Overland Monthly*. Thence to Mexico and Central America, where he held down all kinds of queer jobs and even took part for a brief space in one of the frequently recurring revolutions.

While crossing from Jamaica to San Francisco, Mr. Roberts had stopped off at New York. And felt with an odd conviction that sooner or later he would return to it. And so it happened. In 1911, he was back as the assistant editor of the *National Sunday Magazine*, now dead. A two years' sojourn, and he was off to Paris, landing there with less than $40. But he had no difficulty in connecting with the Paris office of *The Brooklyn Eagle*, and when the war broke out the following August, he became a war correspondent overnight. He was on the battlefield of the first Marne before the fighting ceased, and pushed on with the French forces to the Aisne. Special missions took him many times to the front, and to Spain and England. Interviews with Clemenceau and other Allied leaders brought him to the front rank of correspondents.

In 1919, Mr. Roberts was back in New York, this time as editor of *Ainslee's Magazine*—one of the most interesting jobs he has held, and which kept him put for three years. Following that, there were many adventures to foreign places—to Cuba, Canada, South America, and Europe again.

In 1925, he edited a motion picture fan magazine, *Movie Monthly*. 1926 saw him as publisher and editor of *The American Parade*, the first of the American book-bound quarterlies, and which ran to four volumes. In 1927 he became editor of *The Dance Magazine*, which seems a far cry from his accepted field, but which, in reality, expresses another phase of his versatility. Mr. Roberts has always made a fad of exhibition dancing, especially the Spanish, although he does not dance a step himself. Then, toward the close of 1928, he joined the staff of Harper & Brothers, as editor of *Brief Stories*.

[*The Author & Journalist*, August 1929]

Editors You Want To Know: Captain W.H. Fawcett
Willard E. Hawkins

[Technically, Wilford Hamilton Fawcett (~1895-1940) was the publisher of Fawcett Publications, while his brother, Roscoe (~1887-1936), was managing editor. They both were captains by virtue of their WWI service. Both had previous newspaper experience, W.H. as a reporter with the *Minneapolis Tribune* and city editor of the *Winnipeg Free Press*, Roscoe as sports editor with the Portland *Oregonian*. W.H. returned from the war with a mind full of dirty stories and an idea to cheer up disabled vets. Roscoe had been badly injured in a plane crash near the cliffs of Dover, and that may have been an influence. W.H.'s idea was a little joke book called *Captain Billy's Whiz Bang*, combining W.H.'s nickname with the term for an artillery shell. In the beginning, W.H.'s four sons hauled copies by coaster wagon to local news dealers. The first print order had been for 5000 copies. Within a few years, *Whiz Bang* was selling over 400,000 copies a month, what the *New York Times* called "a gags to riches" story. Roscoe joined him in the business. The success of *Whiz Bang* laid the foundation for a publishing empire. The diversified company published only two pulps, *Triple-X* (later *Triple-X Western*) and *Battle Stories*. Both were 25¢ premium products and remained so, to their detriment, after the stock market crash, when market pressures inevitably depressed most cover prices to 10¢. In early 1932, the company, rethinking its policy, cut back on buying new fiction. The March and May issues of both pulps were skipped. Thereafter, a number of changes ensued. Roger Fawcett, W.H.'s son, and fellow prodigious trapshooter, was promoted to management. The pulps were dropped to 20¢, then enlarged to bedsheet-size, a short-lived experiment that essentially ended the Fawcett pulp line with the November 1932 issues, *Whiz Bang* died in 1932, as well. The two pulps continued through 1936, but only as one-shot reprint annuals. Also, in 1936, Roscoe died. Ralph Daigh, a former pulp editor, took over as managing editor.

"Captain Billy"

In 1940, W.H. succumbed to a heart attack during a bout of pneumonia. The coaster wagon boys took charge of the company—in birth order. W.H., Jr. (~1909-70), the eldest, became president; Roger (~1911-79), general manager; Gordon (~1913-93), treasurer; and Roscoe K. (~1914-??), circulation manager. The company continued to prosper. Prior to the WWII paper shortage, Fawcett published over sixty periodicals. A comic book line was started, with Captain Marvel as the star character. Later, Fawcett Publications diversified into paperbacks, with the successful Gold Medal and Crest labels. They made a fortune off the Peanuts books. In the '70s, they added Ned Pines' Popular Library, the last vestige of the Thrilling empire. In 1977, CBS bought

Fawcett for $50 million, ending the last of the family-owned publishing empires. The three remaining brothers sold out because they were all reaching retirement age, and none of their descendents wanted to take over the company. :: Willard E. Hawkins (1887-1970) founded *The Student-Writer* (January 1916) in Denver, opening that first issue with a "what do editors want?" type of article. He may have had some hint, having already established himself as a freelancer of promise with a 1913 serial in *The Cavalier*. With the October '23 issue, Hawkins' magazine changed title to the more familiar *The Author & Journalist*, which ended up publishing countless articles on the pulps. While editing his magazine, Hawkins continued to publish fiction, always a credibility issue with someone presuming to teach the art. He has the historical distinction of having the first story in the first issue of *Weird Tales* (March 1923), "The Dead Man's Tale." In May 1927, A&J published the first of many articles by Harold Hersey. Hersey returned the favor by publishing many of Hawkins' humorous western shorts in *Western Trails* and other pulps. Many of his western stories featured paired characters like "Chuck and Dingbat" (*Western Rangers*) or "Scoot and Windy" (*Outlaws of the West*). In 1933, he was a founding member of the New York-centered American Fiction Guild and later served as a vice president. In 1940, he sold out his share of A&J to co-owners John T. & Margaret Bartlett, but continued to supply articles and his monthly column *The Student Writer*. In a 1941 piece, "Science Fiction—Newest Pulp Field," he supplied pointers toward cracking that market. Bolstering his advice were a recent string of stories in *Astounding*, *Thrilling Wonder*, and others. In May 1946, he published his last column for A&J, retiring to Craig, Colorado to be closer to his grandkids.]

A BORN BUILDER, Captain W.H. Fawcett has enjoyed the rare experience of never having a magazine failure. A far-sighted anticipation of reader demands, with a faculty for supplying this sometimes fickle audience with what they desire, may account for so happy a record.

When the World War ended, Captain Fawcett foresaw a reaction from the harrowing reality of battle—a swing of the pendulum pushed by thousands upon thousands of soldiers seeking escape from grim memories. His pocket-size magazine, named *Whiz Bang*, after the shells that used to make life exciting for the doughboys, met such a need with rollicking, full-flavored gusto. To this day, a decade after the war, veterans cherish their allegiance to *Whiz Bang*, and it remains the favorite humor magazine of the A.E.F. From this beginning grew the nine magazines now being published by Captain Fawcett.

So phenomenal a success requires more than a consideration of conditions to explain. There is much more to the story than that; back of it is the man himself.

Captain Fawcett is square-shouldered, with the ruddy countenance of your true outdoor sportsman, and with the keen gaze of a champion rifle shot. He was already a veteran when he enlisted for the big fuss across the pond, for he had fought in the Spanish-American War.

During the Philippine engagement, he participated in the war against the Moros in the Mindinao mountains, being stationed across the lake from the encampment where Pershing was a captain. His discharge recorded twenty-seven night attacks, skirmishes, engagements, and campaigns.

A training as a newspaper man proved valuable when Captain Fawcett launched his first venture in the magazine field. He had excelled in sports, was widely travelled, and was favored with a lively, robust sense of humor; a personality that made itself felt in the pages of his publication from the start.

Captain Fawcett's hobbies reflect the spirit of the adventurer. In 1924 he was appointed manager of the American Trapshooting team to compete at the Olympic games in Paris. His team won the World's championship against twelve rivals, and returned with the laurels of victory worn jauntily on their brows. During the Olympics 6500 clay birds whizzed from the traps to test his skill; Captain Fawcett broke 98 per cent of them!

Other evidences of the imprint he has made in American sports may be found in the records of the Sunny South Trapshooting Handicaps, where Captain Fawcett defeated Mark Arie, former World's champion, and Frank Troeh, who has held more records than any other man.

This prowess at the traps is not confined to clay pigeons. Twice he has hunted in Alaska for moose, caribou, mountain sheep, and Kodiak bear. He has hunted in the Canadian Rockies and in the Western States. Trophies of these many hunts hang on the log walls of Breezy Point Lodge, the publisher's retreat in the pines of northern Minnesota. Many more trophies will be added when he returns from his hunting trip to South Africa, planned for next year.

He has built a log home, on the shore of Big Pelican Lake, and Breezy Point has become the "summer capital" of the Fawcett Publications. A constant stream of editors, writers, and visiting notables trek to the Point during the summer. It was here that Sinclair Lewis wrote *Elmer Gantry*.

Headquarters for the Fawcett publications are located in Robbinsdale, a lakeside suburb of Minneapolis, and several of the original farm characters known to *Whiz Bang* fans reside there. Chief Bloberger, the world's most famous constable, still is on the Robbinsdale village payroll, and directed the ceremonies when Tom Mix came to visit Captain Fawcett recently.

Here the other magazines of the string have grown and flourished. *True Confessions*, a pioneer in the field of first-person stories, has given a name to this type of romance until writers universally refer to them as "confession" stories. *Triple-X*, a title devised to cover three of the most popular phases of men's fiction, was launched next. A visit to Hollywood inspired the start of *Screen Secrets*. *Battle Stories* was brought out when it appeared that the public at last was ready to read about war. The prime movement behind *Modern Mechanics*, the latest magazine on the list, was aviation, which has always claimed a major share in Captain Fawcett's interests. *Modern Mechanics* is edited under a plan whereby an expert in each field of mechanics supervises his share of the magazine. Several members of the board of editors are in charge of trade magazines devoted exclusively to their hobbies, and the editor of the airplane division, Major H.H. Arnold, is a veteran army flier and the former assistant chief of the air service during the World War. It is an unusual experiment in magazine editing which is meeting with wide approval.

True Love Affairs publishes first-person mystery stories of the romantic type, and feature articles of diversified interest.

All of Captain Fawcett's magazines pay a minimum of two cents a word on acceptance, with some of the fiction magazines paying as high as ten cents a word. Manuscripts, he insists, shall be reported upon within ten days, and the editorial organization is staffed to follow this rule religiously. Too, a check in payment is sent at the same time the author is notified of an acceptance and writers, therefore, can obtain prompt return on their efforts.

In the offices of the publications hangs this slogan: "*I would rather have less talent than less loyalty.*" Captain Fawcett knows that he must build with reliable material if his work is to endure. That he has always found such loyalty is a criterion of the quality of his leadership.

[*The Author & Journalist*, August 1929]

Editors You Want To Know: Harry E. Maule
William MacLeod Raine

[It's obvious Harry Maule (1886-1971) came from pulp roots. His mother, Mary Katherine Maule, in addition to writing western novels, was a certified pulp writer, having published in *All-Story*, *The Cavalier*, and other magazines. Harry began his career reporting for a hometown paper, *The Denver Times*. Later, he did newspaper work in New York for the *New York Press*; and, in Mexico, worked for *The Mexican Daily Record* and corresponded for *The New York Sun*. In 1906, he became a copy editor for the The United Press in New York. Soon after he joined Doubleday, Page's Country Life Press in 1911, *Short Stories* editor Harry Peyton Steger died suddenly. Maule took over. He gave many writers their start at *Short Stories*, including Ernest Haycox. When the below profile was written, Maule's career was due for some change. He'd been editing *Short Stories*, *West*, and *Frontier Stories*. In 1929, the now-named Doubleday, Doran sold *Frontier* to Fiction House. Scratch one title. Also in '29, as Doubleday, Doran's managing editor, he relinquished *West* to adventure writer Roy de S. Horn. In 1930, de S. Horn took over *Short Stories*, as well, while Maule became more heavily involved in Doubleday's book division. In late '32, de S. Horn went into business for himself, including as consultant to RKO Pictures. Maule returned to supervising *Short Stories*, with Dorothy McIlwraith editing, and *West*, with Edmund Collier editing. Doubleday sold off both titles, the last of their pulps, in the mid-'30s. In 1939, Maule left to become a senior editor with Random House, famously taking his friend Sinclair Lewis with him. Maule reigned as one of New York's most distinguished editors, retiring from Random House in 1966 with a reputation as an authority on the American West—and a great gentleman. Random House chief Bennett Cerf once claimed that Maule's rejection letters made him want to weep. :: William MacLeod Raine (1871-1954) sold his first story in 1898, going on to become a prolific western writer through the first-half of the 20th Century, both in magazines and between hard covers. He sold many stories to Harry Maule for *Short Stories* and *Frontier*, so it's appropriate he would write this profile.]

FOR READERS OF THE AUTHOR & JOURNALIST the Harry E. Maule of whom I write is the one who has long been editor of *Short Stories* and kindred magazines. This is natural enough, since their contacts with him have been through these periodicals. His recent promotion to head of the book department of Doubleday, Doran & Company resulted largely from his success as a magazine editor. It was by most happy chance that this Maule was placed in charge of these magazines, for he has qualified by a remarkable knowledge of the West. More than any editor in New York he is indigenous to the trans-Mississippi country. By birth and inheritance the frontier is in his blood. He has poked his adventurous reportorial nose into a thousand odd corners of it. As Will James says, he knows "a lot of places where a feller can swing his rope and not ketch it on no fence posts." You can't fool Maule with stuff that is not genuine. If it is not true he knows it.

That is one Maule. There is another. In New York Harry Maule derived his importance less because he was editor of *Short Stories* than because he is a valuable asset to the great publishing house with which he is connected. Every time I meet him he has close at hand a book manuscript he expects to read in the small hours after everybody else has gone to bed, one that has to be studied carefully and almost prayerfully, both in justice to Doubleday, Doran & Company and to some struggling young writer whose fate hangs in the balance of the decision to be made. On the book side, before being made chief of that department, Maule was contact man for the house with most of the Western and outdoor writers associated with it, such as Major Frederick R. Burnham, the late Charles M. Russell, Charles Alden Seltzer, Clarence E. Mulford, Walter Noble Burns, and James B. Hendryx, as well as with writers of another genre including Selma Lagerlof, William McFee, and T.S. Stribling. He is a member of the firm and is on the board of directors. Within the space of this article it is not possible even to suggest his activities in the publishing end of his work.

Harry Maule

Harry E. Maule was born in Nebraska July 13, 1886. He was educated in the public schools of Denver and in the East Denver High, then under the guidance of Dr. William H. Smiley.

His father, John Penrose Maule, was a lawyer of the old school, one who believed it to be unethical for a self-respecting man of the law to appear in public without a frock coat and a high silk hat. There is a story about that hat. In Cheyenne, during frontier days, some cowboys caught sight of it in front of a mahogany place of refreshment. They longed for that hat lustily. Their trigger fingers itched to perforate it. They engaged its owner in conversation. He was good humored and smiling, but—the buckaroos decided to seek entertainment elsewhere. John Penrose Maule was a pioneer in Nebraska. He had come there with his parents in a prairie schooner, and there he lived in a sod house, taught school, and studied law. Admitted to the bar before he was 21, he soon became prosecuting attorney for several wild counties, rode the circuit in a buckboard while blizzards swirled about him, and sent various rustlers and murderers to the penitentiary.

It is worth noting that Mary K. Maule, the mother of the editor, was one of the earliest writers of Western fiction. Her book, *Little Knight of the X Bar B*, published more than thirty years ago, antedated *The Virginian* and still sells. Written as a juvenile, it was as popular with adults as with children. Other novels followed this.

So much for background.

Even as a boy Harry Maule was a lover of the outdoors. He spent his summers camping in the mountains of Colorado. He reached them by every known means of transportation—by tramping, by bicycle, by covered wagon, and by saddle horses. He has since been in every western state. Usually when business demands that he go for the house to Europe he compromises on a pack trip to the Flathead River, Montana, or to the Tonto Basin, Arizona. He is an ardent fisherman. He has stalked the rainbow trout on the Gunnison and has fished for bass in Maine. One of the thrills that stays with him is landing a twelve-pound salmon after twilight in a pelting rain on the upper Miramichi, New Brunswick. You will understand that I have space only to touch high spots.

Now about Maule as an editor. To begin with, publishing is a business made possible only by success. This is true of books and it is true of magazines. The prosperity of author and publisher is interdependent. The business is one of small returns, one bound to have many losses. The author must take his chance with the publisher, must be content to share profits reasonably. Maule stays in the publishing and editorial line because he likes good books and stories, and because he loves literature. That is the policy of the house with which he is connected, a policy which he has had some share in shaping. I have had many dealings with Maule, and I have never found him anything but reasonable and fair. We have not always seen eye to eye, but we have always worked out what seemed to both of us an equitable arrangement. In the business world that is all that can be asked for. It may be different in Heaven among the angels.

In his magazines Maule's aim has always been to provide interesting entertainment of a high class with no injurious effect upon the young. He does not yield to the temptation to sacrifice authenticity to melodrama. I claim he knows a good story. When he turns down one of mine he knows exactly why he does it. When he accepts one he can often tell me how it can be improved.

This is true in part because Harry Maule knows his West so well. He reported in Denver in the days of big Bill Heywood of the Western Federation. He drifted to Mexico and reported on Monterrey and Mexico City papers. The adventurous urge took him to New York, where he worked for the United Press and rose to the management of branch bureaus with a staff of correspondents under him. In 1911 he joined Doubleday, Page & Company. In 1912 he was made editor of a sick young magazine child named *Short Stories*. It is now one of the lustiest and best of the whole adventure tribe. Later he conceived and planned *West* and *The Frontier*.

If I reread this sketch I shall know that I haven't given you a picture of Harry Maule at all—of that restless active brain of his, of the slight, tireless figure with the keen, eager eyes that light to a charming smile, of the amazing energy burnt out to lift writers over hard places and make their work presentable. He is one of the hardest workers I know, and a good deal of that work is given to benefit you and me.

But if I wrote the sketch again it probably would not be any nearer the truth. So I'll leave it as it is.

[*The Author & Journalist*, September 1929]

Editors You Want To Know: Daisy Bacon
Joa Humphrey

[Daisy Bacon (~1899-1986) came to New York in the late-'20s, got a part-time bookkeeping job for an auctioneer, and wrote a few pieces on the business, which she sold to *The Saturday Evening Post*. Then she landed an editorial position with Street & Smith's *Love Story Magazine*, in answer to a want ad in the *New York Times*. She'd already been published in the magazine. By mid-'28, she was editor, taking over for Ruth Agnes Abeling. Soon, Bacon was recognized as one of the top editors in the pulps, a female winner in a traditional man's game. Within three years, she raised the circulation to 600,000. They called her "Queen of the Woodpulps." She sat at the big roll-top desk that Theodore Dreiser had used as editor of *Smith's Magazine* decades earlier. *Love Story* was the only weekly woman's magazine in the country; it was a 16-page signature thicker than the other Street & Smith pulps; and Bacon was buying an amazing 500 stories a year. She said: "Because of the trees that have been cut down for all my magazines, I always plant trees whether I am going to stay in the place or not." She's credited with giving many name love-story writers their start. In an April 1934 interview in *The Author & Journalist*, she described the experiences that made her a natural editor: "From the time I was a child I was dissatisfied with the endings in books and magazine stories. As I grew older, I blamed the editors, because it is the editor's business to edit as well as select all stories. I wrote a new ending to *Little Women* when I was fourteen (having Joe marry Laurie), and when they made the movie the other day, I still felt as strongly about it as ever." During her career at S&S, she edited other magazines: *Real Love Magazine*, the revival of *Ainslee's* in 1935 (which turned into *Smart Love Stories*), *Romantic Range*. None duplicated the success of *Love Story*. As the company retrenched in the '40s, she became editor of *Detective Story*. It was her only title after *Love Story* ceased its run with the February 1947 issue. In late '48, after editor Babette Rosmond left the company to raise a family, Bacon inherited *Doc Savage* and *The Shadow* (after a brief interlude from William de Grouchy). Rosmond had governed the digest-era of those magazines. Under Bacon, they were changed to pulp-size quarterlies, giving her the dubious honor of presiding over their final months. She had planned to shift *Doc* more into science fiction, but fans can only wonder what that might have been like. S&S shut down all their pulps in mid-'49 and Bacon was shown the door. Daisy Bacon had written the occasional short story, and the occasional article for the writers' mags. Now she put her wisdom between hard covers: *Love Story Writer* (Hermitage House, 1954). :: Joa Humphrey was a fiction contributor to Daisy Bacon's *Love Story*.]

WHAT DO YOU THINK OF A GIRL who doesn't like caviar, pâté de foie gras, candy, or pie, but eats sugar on lettuce? What is your mental picture of a person who works 12 hours a day, runs her office like a slave driver, but has no personal secretary? How would you rate the ability of one who does all the reading for a weekly magazine and attends to the correspondence which it entails? Would you picture her as blonde, slight, with a low, indistinct voice and a face that should launch at least a hundred ships?

Such, at any rate, is a partial description of Daisy Bacon, editor of *Love Story Magazine*. She is under thirty and sold the first thing she ever wrote to *The Saturday Evening Post*. She was quite successful with popular fiction before she took up editorial work. After a time she went to work for Street & Smith and became editor of a weekly.

Daisy Bacon

She is a keen businesswoman and has a mind that works like lightning. In fact, Miss Bacon has made her living in three other businesses besides that of author and editor. One of her boasts is that she can make her living at anything.

She gives quick decisions on manuscripts, and often returns a story to the author with instructions as to how to fix it. Her associates claim that she remembers everything. She has the weirdest possible collection of facts at her fingertips. She can locate anything in her roll-top desk immediately, although it always looks as if the overflow from it would envelop her at any time. She either has a closet full of clothes or none at all.

She hates hot weather although she never looks hot; never loses her temper; likes cats, turtles and elephants. Her idea of a good time is to put on a pair of overalls and fuss around in the hot sun in the flower garden. As for her literary tastes, she likes Louis Bromfield, Elmer Davis, *The Saturday Evening Post* and—of course—*Love Story Magazine!*

[*The Author & Journalist*, November 1929]

Editors You Want To Know: Edwin Baird
MacKinley Kantor

[Few pulp personalities rival the longevity of Edwin Baird (1886-1957), both as writer and editor. His stories appeared in *All-Story* as early as 1910; in the final years of his life, he had a series of shorts in *The Saint Detective Magazine* digest (mid-'50s). Despite his many accomplishments, he's probably best-remembered for a failure, editing *Weird Tales* in its first year of existence (March 1923 to April 1924) (along with its companion pulp, *Detective Tales*). In *Weird Tales*, Baird published a veritable who's-who of memorable writers: H.P. Lovecraft, Clark Ashton Smith, Vincent Starrett, Seabury Quinn. However, the magazine lost money. Publisher J.C. Henneberger sold off *Detective Tales* (and *College Humor*), and Baird went with the deal. He edited newly-named *Real Detective Tales* into the early-'30s when it converted to a true-crime mag. A 1925 solicitation for *RDT* made the magazine sound pretty exciting: "I am in the market now for dramatic short stories . . . that hum with tense action and suspense—vivid, thrilling stories in which every word counts and that will keep the reader breathlessly interested to the last sentence."

Edwin Baird

Arthur J. Burks, who sold his first detective stories to Baird, wrote: "Baird belongs in my portrait gallery of understanding editors." Tom Curry also had fond memories: "Baird would buy half a dozen stories from me at once, and run them in the same issue under pseudonyms." Baird was well-known for reading all submissions himself, sans assistants. Agent August Lenniger wrote: "Edwin Baird's cryptic blue-penciled two-and-three-word criticisms have been like so many diamonds to many mystery writers." But Frank Gruber had a less than happy experience with Baird, as he described in *The Pulp Jungle*: "Edwin Baird made a big thing in the back of the magazine about his writers. He was always 'discovering' new writers and he welcomed them to his magazine. I took a day off from my regular job and went down to see Mr. Baird. I got into his office, all right, but he kept me standing and gave me about thirty seconds of his valuable time. I handed him a manuscript. I will say this, he sent it back with a personal note—instead of the familiar rejection slip. The substance of the note was 'forget it.' " After *RDT*, Baird tried to establish a new magazine, *Real America*. It didn't last long. He'd been publishing fiction all through his editing years, and in the mid-'30s he began hitting the slicks, appearing in *Esquire* and *Liberty*. His byline became commonplace in the burgeoning true-crime market. But he never ventured too far from the crime *fiction* magazines. :: MacKinley Kantor (1904-77) became famous as an author of historical fiction, particularly about the Civil War, including the Pulitzer Prize-winning *Andersonville* (1955). But he started his career as a pulp writer, selling many of his early stories to

Baird's *RDT*, then later *Clues* and *Detective Fiction Weekly*. By 1935, he was well-established as a slick-magazine writer, appearing in *The Saturday Evening Post*, *Liberty*, *Collier's*, and many others.]

ANY WEEK-DAY OF THE YEAR, if you enter the yellow brick building at the blind end of Maple street, in Chicago, and climb two flights of stairs to the third floor, you are apt to find Edwin Baird, editor of *Real Detective Tales*, literally up to his waist in work.

In a rear office suite of the Collegiate World Publishing Company, separated by only a hall from *Real Detective Tales'* flapper sister, *College Humor*, this blue-eyed ex-newspaperman hammers his typewriter, wields a ruthless blue pencil and daily wades through a stack of manuscripts before which the heart of any ordinary professional reader would quail. And does he like it? Say!

Baird is no misfit, would-be writer who has landed in an editorial job because of inaptitude at the profession of his dreams. With three successful novels and hundreds of magazine stories behind him, he is doing what he enjoys doing: putting out a detective and crime-story magazine that is the head of its class. He has all the enthusiastic energy of a youngster, which reflects itself in the bantering, breezy and cynical tone of his monthly editorials.

The trail which brought him to the editorial chair of *RDT* began down in Tennessee some forty years ago, and led through the local rooms of small-town and big-town dailies, through courts and morgues and gambling dens, all of which he saw with the wide-awake eyes of a police reporter. Baird has seen men shot down and watched gang hang-outs being raided; he has hurtled along crowded streets in detective squad cars; he has been the confidant of condemned men who waited for the rope in shadowy cells. . . . I would like to see an over-ambitious writer slip any fake crook stuff over on him!

Not long ago the editor of one of the most influential literary magazines took a long, sad tumble when he featured the hobo stories of a writer who drenched his scenes with the most fantastic detail, absurd to any reader who knew the reality of a bum's life. . . . It would be an impossibility to victimize Edwin Baird in a similar fashion. Baird *knows*.

No aspiring short-story writer could have a better friend than this genial, quick-moving editor. The saga of his "finds," good turns and philanthropies would fill many pages. Does a young writer enter his office with a manuscript, and beg an audience? . . . Well, he won't be sent away without a hearing.

"Yes, I *am* busy. . . . But that's all right. Sit down. What have you got? Story for me? Let's see it."

He works as he talks, in brief, assured gestures. And if any man—or woman—expect to have a cargo of applesauce given him or her by reason of a personal call, he or she had better shed the illusions.

"Sorry. Couldn't use this at all. This first page alone would kill it for us. . . .

Got anything else? . . . Better luck next time!"

Big names, although he buys plenty of them, cannot dim Baird's perception for any good story, no matter how unsung its author. Nothing can give him the joy that a real discovery does. I have seen him wildly jubilant over finding one convincing, well-done yarn in a ton of shoddy, disorganized and often plagiarized manuscripts.

"Read this, will you? . . . Isn't that a good story? You bet, I'm buying it! . . . No, I never heard of the author before. New to me. New to everybody, perhaps. But he can write!"

His luxurious apartment on the lake front, with its unsurpassed view of Lake Shore Drive, is the Mecca of fiction writers, editors, newspaper men. It is here that Baird does much of his voluminous reading, and here that many manuscripts are weighed for acceptance, or sent back "into the woods" for permanent exile. . . . Suppose one drops in on the editor of *RDT* at eleven o'clock some Saturday evening. He may find Layng of the *Daily News* and Babcock of the *Tribune* engaged in an amiable game of chess; Vincent Starrett and Harry Stephen Keeler in one corner, discussing British agents; Jack Woodford, Snowshoe Al Bromley and Merlin Taylor in another, discussing prohibition (in no uncertain terms); "Bunker" Bean of *Hygiea* coaxing college songs from the grand piano. . . . And moving from chess to British agents with equal assurance, pausing to nudge the discussers of prohibition, and dropping over to join in the chorus with Bean, is Ed, the editor and host. He plays with as much energy as he works, and that is saying something.

He has a particular aversion to stories which begin, "Inspector Burke picked up the receiver," or " 'No,' said the old native, 'Nobody's lived in that house for fifty years. Folks say as how it's haunted.' " . . . He wears his hat all the time he is in his office. . . . When Baird's novel, *The City of Purple Dreams* [1913], was purchased for the cinema, it commanded the highest price which had ever been paid for motion picture rights of a novel, at that time. . . . No manuscript is ever rejected by *Real Detective Tales* until the editor himself has read at least part of it. . . . At some period every summer, Baird vanishes into the lake-dotted wilderness of the north, and comes out with a red mustache and a long string of fish-stories. . . . His own novels, published in Europe, have received much acclaim. . . . He goes for long walks every Sunday, and ragged children in the slums are forever guessing at the identity of the good-natured man who treated them all to ice-cream and then took them for a row on the park lagoon. . . . Baird spends infinite time and care in the selection of his magazine covers; they *must* suit; cover artists toil indefatigably to please him. . . . He hates machinery and refuses to own an automobile. . . . He has been known to order, read, accept and pay for a story by an impoverished but talented young writer, all within twenty-four hours. . . . He is happily married, and his wife aids him in many unofficial phases of his work. . . . For recreation, Edwin Baird reads much non-fiction: scientific works, astronomical and explorative in tone. . . . If you submit a manuscript to him, never accompany it with a letter stating: "All my friends tell me this is a good story," or, "Although my name may mean nothing to you, I am already quite well-known in California." If this sketch hasn't made the reason clear, just take my word for it.

[*The Author & Journalist*, January 1930]

Editors You Want To Know: Lawrence Lee

[Lawrence Lee (1903-78) succeeded A.L. Sessions as editor of *Sea Stories* and *Sport Story* in mid-'27. When *Sea Stories* changed to *Excitement* with the July 1930 issue, Lee remained editor, but by the end of the year he returned to his alma mater, the University of Virginia, to teach English and French. He published his first book of poetry, *Summer Goes On*, in 1933. He joined the Navy in WWII, and after his service returned to academia at the University of Pittsburgh.]

LAWRENCE LEE IS A NATIVE OF ALABAMA. He obtained his schooling in Montgomery, Alabama, and his first interest in poetry began at Sidney Lanier High School of that city.

Later he graduated from the University of Virginia. There he wrote for the *University of Virginia Magazine* and during his college years contributed poetry to various poetry magazines, finally appearing in larger magazines at the end of university years.

During his last year at the University he edited the University magazine. His work has appeared in *The American Mercury, Scribner's, Harper's, The Nation, Bookman, Century, Books (Herald-Tribune), Saturday Review, Virginia Quarterly Review*, and others, as well as in several anthologies, including Jessie B. Rittenhouse's *Third Book of Modern Verse*.

His editorial work in New York, as he expresses it, includes a brief term as office boy under Mr. S.S. McClure, an opener of letters about colic and babies' layettes for *The People's Home Journal*, a reporter of sorts and a worse critic for *Musical America*, and an editorial assistant under the late Mr. A.L. Sessions, his predecessor in the present position.

Mr. Lee says: "It was my work with Mr. A.L. Sessions which seems the most valuable that I have done, from the standpoint of training. He had back of him a distinguished career when it was my good fortune to obtain a position with him. His career never lacked distinction. He was one of the splendid group of good editors who have always needed patience, vision, and gentleness—and, at times, courage. He had these qualities in their healthiest forms. What few things I have done in writing owe some quality of good to such influences as Mr. Sessions and his friendship.

"Mr. Charles Agnew MacLean, lately deceased, was another fine editor with whom I had some contact. He had a powerful mind when he once determined upon what purpose he would set it; and that purpose was filled with clear-cut justice. I did not know him at the height of his career; but his career was never undistinguished. There are now many writers who feel severely the absence of his aid and friendship. Like Mr. Sessions, who had guided and befriended such celebrated figures as O. Henry, Mr. MacLean gave aid to many important fiction writers.

"With these memories of men who could edit with a largeness of mind and spirit, I have tried to turn in to the pages of *Sport Story Magazine* and *Sea Stories* as much insight and creative enthusiasm as possible.

"Many writers and friends of mine have asked how I could be interested in trying to write good poetry on one hand and in editing popular fiction magazine on the other. At one time I might have joined them in their questions. Now the two works do not seem at all diverse. If I could write with unsentimental honesty the poetry that is alive in football, track, swimming, or such poetry as there is in the sea, I should be a great poet.

"*Sport Story Magazine* is open for literature as great as any that the world has known. It is, of course, for many reasons, hardly probable that this magazine will receive one of the world's masterpieces. Yet, it will continue to be an honest, clean, entertaining publication; and it will always be looking for good sport stories—even as good, say, as Kipling's 'Maltese Kitten.'

"The same is the case with *Sea Stories*. We look for greatness, as well as entertaining fiction. If we have only found goodness as well as entertaining fiction, this far along the way, nothing has been lost. There have been small victories. We have won prizes for stories, and we have published some of the very excellent contemporary poets and short-story writers, and writers of good long fiction.

"In both magazines we shall continue to welcome with joy any young writer who shows promise or present achievement. Big names are, naturally, valuable; but good work is more valuable. We can always use good work. If we fail to see it when it is submitted, that is our misfortune; and such a failure is not intentional. We shall continue to look with hope and energy."

[*The Author & Journalist*, August 1930]

Editors You Want to Know: Harriet A. Bradfield
B. Virginia Lee

[Harriet Alma Bradfield's (~1899-1953) magazine career began in the early-'20s, although the specifics are not clear beyond the below profile. She came to New York from Wisconsin; lived alone in Greenwich Village for the duration. She published verse under the name Jeanne Stewart, and perhaps some fiction. *Author & Journalist* never listed her as named editor for *Cupid's Diary*, so she probably assisted one or more of the other four editors who ran the magazine from 1923 through late-'28. At that time, Bradfield became editor of *Love Romances* for Fiction House, a job she held until the pulp was suspended after the April 1932 issue with the death of J.B. Kelly, Treasurer and head of Fiction House. For her next job, she joined *Writer's Digest* to supply the monthly column, *New York Market Letter*, replacing Joseph Lichtblau who inaugurated the column in the January '32 issue. Bradfield's first column appeared in October '32. In 1933, she became editor of a new Popular Publications pulp, *Lovers Magazine*, while continuing to compose the *Market Letter*. *Lovers Magazine* came on the market the same month, October 1933, as three other Popular titles: *The Spider*, *G-8 and His Battle Aces*, and *Star Western*. "In writing for this market," Bradfield advised, "keep in mind that the simpering Cinderella type of heroine is not wanted. Modern, intriguing types who know their way around, who live vividly and love dangerously, make better story material." As for October '33, three out of four ain't bad—if you're the publisher. *Lovers Magazine* folded after five issues while the others went on to long life. "The love field has been finding the going very bad," Bradfield concluded sadly in the *Market Letter*. While continuing with the column, she stayed involved with the "sub-slick field," as she called it, publishing many romantic poems under her own name; the short little one and two-stanza types used as page-filler at the end of stories. But despite her creative impulses, Bradfield's legacy would be the *New York Market Letter*, which she wrote to the end of her life. Renowned for its strong factual reporting, the column was a chronicle of happenings in the magazine markets, especially the pulps, and continues to yield valuable historical information available nowhere else. The April 1953 *Writer's Digest* ran the *Market Letter*, as usual, under her byline, but the words were not her own: "The phone call came at 4:40 p.m., Thursday, March 19, as we were putting the April issue to bed. Harriet A. Bradfield is dead." :: B. Virginia Lee edited the *Overland Monthly* circa 1926. She seems to have clicked with Harold Hersey. They co-edited the non-fiction journal *Famous Lives* (1929). Later, her fiction appeared in his pulps, *Quick Trigger Western* and *Riders of the Range*.]

WHO SAYS THE EDITOR NEVER SEES the stories mailed in to the magazine? Here's one who does. Harriet A. Bradfield, managing editor of *Love Romances*, insists on doing her own first reading and gets a huge kick out of attacking a mountainous Monday morning mail. The letters accompanying manuscripts always interest her intensely. But she likes to know her writers and interprets the letters according to the personalities revealed. Feminine writers afford her special amusement when they address her as "Mr." and attempt a flirtation in order to put stories across.

Her very serious blue eyes belie the good nature and vivid sense of humor lurking beneath. She is rather quiet, preferring that you do the talking—unless she knows you very well, or you hit one of her pet subjects such as French *hors d'oeuvres* in their native habitat.

Usually she keeps darkly shadowed the fact that she was once induced to teach English literature and story writing in a high school and begins the tale of her career in the advertising department of *True Story Magazine*. From there she shifted into the editorial department, and then jumped to the editorship of *Cupid's Diary*. The constant procession of ocean liners slipping down North River, which could be seen from her desk, proved too luring and she resigned in favor of going to Europe. Now she presides over the fate of stories sent to *Love Romances*.

She is a "typical" New Yorker, having come from the Middle West and fallen victim to the lure of the city, especially to its theaters. She loves any and every kind of play, and has written and directed an historical pageant and amateur productions ranging from vaudeville stunts to a musical comedy.

According to her, the baby grand piano is the only important piece of furniture in her apartment—but she has to shut the windows in order to keep out the neighbors' violent protests. The waffle iron is second most important—with good reason!

And she wishes the day were at least twice as long so that she would have time to read all the new books, see all the shows on Broadway, and write a lot herself.

[*The Author & Journalist*, August 1930]

Editors You Want to Know: A.H. Bittner
B. Virginia Lee

[Archibald H. Bittner—Archie—was an experienced adventure-pulp editor, as discussed below. But in the '30s, his career shot off at an unusual tangent. He followed his *Argosy* service with a stint at Dell Publishing, editing *Western Romances* and *War Stories*. And then nothing. Excepting a March 1938 article in *Writers' Markets and Methods*, "A.H. Bittner" fell off the map. As pulp magazine historian Will Murray has discovered, Bittner ran into some legal trouble, then resurfaced as a Thrilling staffer, then as the prolific weird menace author, Wayne Rogers. Murray lays out the sordid and fascinating saga in "Archie Bittner and The Spider: The Case of the Missing 'Master'" (*Blood 'n' Thunder*, Spring 2005).]

WRITERS MAY BE BORN, not made, though experience seems to point otherwise, but turning to editors we are on sure ground. The men who guide the destinies of magazines must have a grounding of experience in order to assemble the contents that cause circulation to become healthy and stay that way. Harry E. Maule, for years editor of the Doubleday, Doran magazines, trained able assistants. One of these is A.H. Bittner, who has for the last two years taken over the editorship of the *Argosy* magazine.

Here is one of the oldest fiction magazines in the country, selling at only ten cents. To compete with the fifteen, twenty and twenty-five cent all-fiction, Mr. Bittner must have figured that the first thing to do was not only to keep old favorites, but to go after the big-timers who were being featured on the other fellows' covers. So he gathered in feature fiction by such stars as Frank L. Packard, H. Bedford-Jones, J. Allan Dunn, Talbot Mundy, and other favorites. Thus old readers are kept, and new ones obtained.

Editors today tend to specialize in particular types of short stories. To Mr. Bittner no type is barred, except the sex angle. Adventure, crime, mystery, railroad, circus, air, West, exotic, sea, war, and humor; all kinds, in fact, if they have rapid-fire action and masculine appeal.

In criticism, Mr. Bittner may be said to be keen, ruthless, yet at the same time constructive. He can pick a story to pieces as if it were a no-account puzzle with weak points, yet he is suggestive in putting his fingers on plot possibilities that may be strengthened if there is anything there to work on.

The popular idea of an editor is a chap sitting back and going over the varied contributions that come in the daily mail. This would be taking things as they come. A.H. Bittner has a policy of his own. Part of his day is spent in interviewing authors, putting out feelers for the kind of material he wants, balancing future magazine contents so they will have the expected appeal. Merely finding new blood, new authors, is of course a part of an up-to-date editor's job, but it isn't the greatest part by a long shot. A "discovery" is thrilling, but it doesn't happen every day, or every month.

The qualities of judgment and appraisal of public appeal come from the fruits of experience. So it is that A.H.'s success is partly accounted for by a background.

Mr. Bittner first worked as an associate editor on several small weeklies, then as a newspaper reporter on the Madison *Eagle* and the New York *Globe*. Then he went to *Adventure*, as assistant to Arthur Sullivant Hoffman, and stayed for three years. Called by Harry E. Maule to *Short Stories*, he was an associate editor on that magazine for a period, and then took over *Frontier*. From the last named magazine he came to the editorship of *Argosy*.

Instead of being apologetic as regards the literary value of the woodpulps, Mr. Bittner is militant in arguing in their cause. He asserts that better and liver fiction appears in the all-fictions than in the magazines that comprise some of the so-called quality group. Recently, on a vacation, he had to fall back on several magazines of the last-named field for reading matter—and was frankly bored. He maintains that it is harder to break into *Argosy* than into various of the illustrated periodicals.

Alive and alert, with the habit of quick decision, Mr. Bittner certainly would be taken rather for a business executive of the more forceful type than a desk worker. Indeed, in his office, he is often on his feet, nervous and prone to emphasis, full of enthusiasm or as ready in dispraise. Possessed of these vivid qualities, he likes speed and movement in fiction, characters on their toes, and plots that get somewhere. In favoring this type of fiction he reflects the bulk of American readers, and perhaps that is a very natural reason why *Argosy* has been forging ahead since he took the wheel.

[*The Author & Journalist*, October 1930]

Editors You Want to Know: Farnsworth Wright
E. Hoffmann Price

[Of Farnsworth Wright (1988-1940), little needs to be said here. He remains one of the most revered pulp editors, for his influential reign at *Weird Tales* (November 1924 to March 1940); in addition to the well-remembered, but unsuccessful, *Oriental Stories* (October/November 1930 - Summer 32) and *The Magic Carpet Magazine* (January 1933 - January 1934). :: Edgar Hoffmann Price (1898-1988) sold his first story to *Weird Tales* in 1925, at the start of a long and productive career in the pulps. A detailed account of his relationship with Wright can be found in the Price collection, *Book of the Dead* (Arkham House, 2001).]

"FIRST OF ALL," declared Farnsworth Wright as he shooed from the editorial rooms of *Weird Tales* a handful of loitering ghouls, vampires, and ghosts, "I insist upon there being a story. Authors only too often confuse story material or story setting with the story itself. The transplanting of a human brain into the skull of an ape would be an interesting surreal experiment; but a tale based on such a feat is acceptable only when the results of the transplanting are dramatic and striking.

"The pseudo-scientific story which is now so much in demand must do more than outline a fanciful invention or process entirely beyond the reach of present scientific achievement. The author must develop a plot which derives its major interest not from the pseudo-scientific principle itself but from an ingenious solution based on a startling application of that principle.

"Tales which carry the hero to distant planets come to my desk by the score. But in most cases the characters, after having been projected into interstellar space, experience commonplace adventures they could much more readily have found on earth.

"Ghost stories of the right kind are welcomed; but we invariably reject those which describe nothing but the terror inspired by the mere appearance of a ghost. These are old-fashioned. When Sir Walter Scott wrote "The Tapestried Chamber," he gave a splendid example of a ghost story in which nothing happened except that someone was frightened almost to death because he saw a ghost. If a ghost story is to make the grade, it must possess motivation and characterization rather than be a rubber-stamped catalogue of wails, apparitions, and clammy hands.

"Again, a weird tale must be convincing. Because we use stories that are frankly impossible, authors are surprised when their work is rejected as not being plausible. The point is that while a concededly impossible hypothesis can be accepted by the reader, the story is satisfying only if the sequence of events based on the impossible is logical and consistent. We can accept a ghost, a vampire, or an evil spirit only when unusual and dramatic action rather than mere presence is the substance of the story. The supernatural as such is by no means adequate; and since we deal with the impossible, it is all the more necessary that they should be convincing; that they should *seem* real.

"We have printed tales of vampires vividly and humanly characterized instead of being obscured by a time-worn litany of garlic and holly sprigs; and we have presented stories whose point was not the personal appearance of Satan, but rather his unusual reaction to a startling and dramatic situation. There are truly great weird tales, which, through their scarcity, are always in demand.

"Finally, our ideal is the presentation of a story having literary value. Very often we accept a tale which though not emphasizing the weird, the supernatural, or the pseudo-scientific, merits approval on account of its rich color, exquisite workmanship, bizarre philosophy, and strong plot."

Now let us turn from quotation to a sketch of the man himself:

Farnsworth Wright tumbled into the magazine business before he was out of grammar school in San Francisco, where he not only wrote and edited a publication called *The Laurel*, but set the type and printed it on a hand press, being editor, author, printer's devil, compositor, and pressman.

During his last two semesters in college he was managing editor of the University of Washington *Daily*. After graduation he was a reporter for the Chicago *Tribune*, and the Chicago *Herald-Examiner*, and later, music critic of the last named. He then left the newspaper game to edit a magazine called *Health*, whose brief career was soon ended by the untimely death of the publisher.

While occupied as reporter and editor, Wright was selling stories to *Munsey's* and other magazines. When *Weird Tales* made its appearance, he sold material which appeared in its initial issues; and later, he read manuscripts for both *Weird Tales* and *Detective Tales*. Shortly thereafter, when the Popular Fiction Publishing Company took over *Weird Tales*, he became publisher. He is now launching a new magazine, *Oriental Stories*.

Thus, baldly sketched, we have his history. But those who have heard its ups and downs from Wright himself when coffee and cigars follow dinner at Le Petit Gourmet, not far from the editorial rooms on Michigan Boulevard, can best understand why "Pious Plato" goes to such pains to encourage promising beginners: for in each beginner Wright sees himself again fighting his way from ham and eggs. Personal rejections, accompanied by bits of constructive criticism, have made of a good many beginners prime members of Wright's circle of chronic contributors. Wright, the editor, is first and last the friend of the author.

Wright served during the World War as an interpreter in the A.E.F. His repertoire, in addition to French, includes Spanish, German, Italian, and a touch of Russian; all of which is an outcropping of his taste for the foreign and colorful. Kouskous, pilau, and East Indian curry are his favorite dishes; Latakia and Darjeeling suit his tastes, respectively, in tobacco and tea; and when he's thirsty . . . well, he mixes an unusually fragrant drink with Bacardi, limes, and pineapple juice as the basic principles.

As to his personal appearance: a cubistic painter has given us a portrait which depicts Wright as the editor of a ghoulish magazine should, but does not look.

Finally, his favorite weakness must be mentioned: limericks!

"Farnsworth, recite the one about the young man from Bombay."

[*The Author & Journalist*, November 1930]

Shooting at the Moon
Wallace R. Bamber

[Bamber slings it straight here—maybe too straight. It's doubtful the ambitious readers of A&J wanted to hear about the days when the irritable editor doesn't open any of the manuscripts that come in the mail. In remarks published in *Writer's Digest* a month earlier, he'd said, "Are we open to stories by new writers? Beginning with December we are going to use at least one story in each issue by a writer who has never sold before." So far so good; but then: "We want the kind of stories that H. Bedford-Jones writes. Another writer whose stories we like is Theodore Roscoe, and another is J. Allan Dunn. The new writer who can turn out stories like these men will meet with a ready reception in our office." What was a freelancer to think? The door is wide-open—as long as I can write like the top names in the field. Bamber broke into the pulps about 1928, appearing in a wide variety of war titles, everything from *War Birds* to *War Stories*. He seems to have had uncanny bad luck hitting war pulps that came and went in a hurry: *Under Fire Magazine*, *Eagles of the Air*, *Complete Aviation Novel Magazine*, etc. Perhaps that's what finally prompted a career shift. "For several years I've wanted to publish a magazine," he said, "but I waited until I found an idea that clicked with me. Then a friend mentioned the appeal of stories of the Far East and I jumped at it." The result was *Far East Adventure Stories*. He entered into talks with Bedford-Jones, who offered to write the entire first issue—at 6¢ a word. Bamber declined the offer, which probably would have busted him at half the price. At any rate, he wrote HBJ that if the first three issues sold well, he'd have him write the entire fourth issue—all under his own name. It never happened. *Far East*, launched with ads and fanfare, never really got off the ground. It ran for seven consecutive monthly issues, starting with October 1930. The March and April 1931 issues included editorials by Bamber, co-signed by assistant Anatole Feldman, appealing to readers to encourage their friends to support the magazine, and announcing a nickel price-drop to 20¢. After the April issue, the schedule became erratic. The last issue was dated February 1932. A&J published a lengthy article by Bamber in the July 1932 issue ("Let's Face the Facts, Pulp Writers!," reprinted in *Pulp Fictioneers*), a somewhat pessimistic view of the future of the pulps. The article was met with a number of stern rebuttals, unusual for the normally uncontroversial writers' mags. But Bamber's prediction that word-rates were down to stay proved prophetic. Immediately after *Far East* failed, Bamber's stories started appearing in the Thrilling pulps, mostly *Thrilling Adventures*, but also an appearance in *Thrilling Detective*. In early '34, he appeared in *Conflict*, another doomed pulp. Then in 1934-35, he started showing up in the back of Street & Smith hero pulps, *Doc Savage* and *Pete Rice*. But that closed out his pulp career. The record is incomplete, but at this point he appears to have had four non-overlapping "careers" in seven years: war pulp author, adventure pulp publisher, Thrilling contributor, Street & Smith contributor. Did he have an "outspokenness problem" with editors he was selling to, or, in the end, was it just about the money? "I am a cold-blooded writer who writes for profit and nothing else," he proclaims at the end of this piece. He moved to Seattle in early '35. He'd been an active member of the New York-based American Fiction Guild which organized writers, editors, and publishers, most having ties to the pulps. The AFG bulletins provide us with the last scraps of information on Bamber. In June 1936, he was still writing and trying to organize a Seattle chapter of the AFG. By 1937, that effort was in hibernation.]

Wally Bamber

YES, SHOOTING AT THE MOON. It is a rather pleasing diversion, but no one ever gets anywhere by doing it. All the moon rockets and high explosive gadgets that have been aimed at that celestial body have come right back to this old earth of ours and nary a one has come anywhere near the moon. I don't say that one may not hit some day—but that will be after our time. What I am concerned with now is the present, and every aspiring writer that pens for profit and not glory should be concerned with the same era—the red hot present. The future will take care of itself.

Stories that are written for possible sale to the magazines of the present day should not be aimed at the moon. If they are, they come right back to the place they started from. And nobody yet has invented any use for rejection slips that makes their keeping worth while. Dollars are the only returns that count to the man or woman who writes for profit. And the easiest way to get the dollars is to start in sharpshooting. Let the more romantic souls who write for expression's sake do all the shooting at the moon. You who are trying to write for profit needn't worry about their hitting it either, and knocking it out of the skies so you can't use it in your stories. It has been shot at many millions of times and the surface isn't even dented yet.

For some unknown reason, the amateur writer persists in writing the story *he* wants to write, rather than the story the editor wants him to write. I haven't been an editor long, but the flock of manuscripts I receive here in the editorial offices of *Far East Adventure Stories* is no different, I know, from the mass of them that go to other editorial offices. And while my magazine has a title that is certainly descriptive of the kind and locale of the stories it contains, that title seemingly means nothing to many writers who are trying to crash the gates for profit. I get every kind of a story under the sun and they are set everywhere on the face of this earth and a lot of other earths I never heard of.

Another symptom of the moon shooter shows up when I open up a story and plunge right into a mad love scene in the beginning paragraph. Yet, *Far East* is purely an adventure magazine. Woman interest, if there is any at all, must be entirely subordinate to the story plot-and-action sequences. The author usually writes that there is a mad love angle to the story, but it was sent along anyway because it was laid in Africa, India, or even Colombia; and excuses that last by saying that Colombia is just as good a spot for adventure as any country in the Far or Near East. And right there is where the editor begins to get mad and tear at his hair—if he has any left. The author shows, by the written letter attached to the manuscript, that he does know your requirements, but along comes the shot at the moon, anyway.

Such a deluge of manuscripts by the moon-shooters has contributed very much to conditions that exist in various editorial offices today, conditions that have been hinted at before, perhaps, by other writers in THE AUTHOR & JOURNALIST. But I am sure they have never before been more than hinted at, perhaps for the reason that most editors don't want to loosen their tongues too much, for fear of losing their jobs. I have no such fear, for I happen to be the publisher of *Far East*, so I am going to place the cards up on the table, in order that all who read this article may know as much about these conditions as I do. And knowing about them may do much to rectify them. For until they are rectified, it is going to become increasingly difficult for new writers to crash the gates.

"Now just what is this bombshell he is about to explode?" you are probably thinking. Namely this: That editors are human and get tired like every other workman. And sometimes they get so darned tired of wading through the trash that comes into their offices in every mail that they give up in disgust and don't read any of it.

"Ah—Oh!" I can hear you readers gasping now. "But how does he get the stories to fill his magazine then, if he doesn't read any of the manuscripts that come in?"

Easy as pie, dear reader, easy as pie. He orders them from known authors with whom he has done business before, and saves himself all the trouble of wading through the batch of manuscripts that the moon-shooters shoot in.

If that is true, you are going to ask how conditions are going to be rectified, and where there is a spot for the new writer to crash in. I am going to try to answer both parts of that query.

Start at the bottom, especially you beginner, and watch closely the trend of the fiction market. New magazines are still coming out every month or so, and this last month of September has seen nearly a dozen make their maiden appearance on the now overcrowded newsstands of the country. There rests the best market for all beginners, and you should shoot at it. Not generally, but specifically.

The new magazine usually operates on a small editorial budget, therefore it is impossible for the editor to go out and buy stories from the better known professionals—their word rates are too high for him to pay. And secondly, he hasn't had time to gather a writing coterie around him yet, which he will do, sure as shootin', if the magazine is a success, and the moon-shooters keep piling trash into his offices. There is the open sesame for amateur writers who are trying to worm into the professional class. Pick on a new magazine, and *sharpshoot*. Get the first issue, read every story in it religiously, then sit down and write one just like those you have read, and you will find that the way past the editor is not at all impossible, nor even highly improbable. In fact, you might be agreeably surprised by getting a check for your very first effort. Of course the check won't be a big one, such as H. Bedford-Jones might get, but it will be a check, and that is something in this day of falling markets and hard times.

The editor wants stories by new writers for that very reason—if they are down his alley. The low word rate he pays beginners brings his editorial costs down, and enables him to save a few extra dollars to go out and get a top-notch professional for his lead story. There is the one spot where the beginner has more than an even chance of crashing the gates of profit. But if you insist on shooting at the moon, you will throw even that one chance away. If the editor of the new magazine finds his desk piled high with manuscripts he can't use, or even think of using, he, too, is going to get disgusted and throw his hands high in the air in surrender. He will send out letters to well-known writers and ask them if they have any stories on hand to sell at a low word rate. And despite what may be said about most professionals having stories unsold, usually such letters bring forth a few well-worn rejects. The stories may not be good, but they carry the well-known author's name, and that counts heavily when the magazine goes on sale.

Now that I have spoken my piece generally, I'll get down to the task specifically. I said to watch the fiction market trends. One year the Western story is in the ascendancy, the next year the War or Air story comes up to steal the peak. At other times it is the Detective or Gangster Story, or the Adventure yarn that is most in demand.

It takes no sage or man of wisdom to determine which one is in the ascendancy. The easily read barometer is before you at all times. Watch the new magazines that come out and see what class they fall into. Then pick out one of them and start sharpshooting.

A few years ago, after Lindbergh's flight, we witnessed the dynamic rush of the Air story to the top of the heap. A short time before that, it was the demand for War stories that had all the professionals writing at top speed to supply the calls for that distinctive type. This last year has seen the resumptions of demand for Western stories, and the rise of the Detective yarn to the highest peak it has yet assumed.

The Love story goes on forever like Tennyson's brook, and has very few bumps, either up or down. It is the one market that remains comparatively steady while all others tend to fluctuate sharply. And for that reason it is not such fertile stamping ground for the new writer. But right now, when the Detective story has reached its peak and begun to recede, is the faint intimation of the rise of the Adventure story, and the very blatant shriek of the Gangster type yarn, which is no more like the old deductive style Detective yarn than this article is like one of Kipling's gems.

These last two markets afford the best chance for the beginning writer right here at present. Next year it may be, and probably will be, something else, but we have already decided to let the future take care of itself, and concern ourselves with the present—the red-hot present.

In the Gangster field, there are, I believe, about eight magazines: *The Underworld Magazine*, which is the oldest; *Gangster Stories*, *Gangland Stories*, *Racketeer Stories*, *Detective-Dragnet*, *Gang World*, *Gun Molls*, and *Prison Stories*. Most of these differ in type. A story that will fit in one of them will not always fit in the other. So a writer, when he sits down to write a gang story, should not just write a gang story—in other words, shoot at the moon. He should pick out the magazine he intends to aim at and write a story for it, just like the ones he read in the issue at hand. And by no means should he write a story until he has read a complete issue of the magazine he is shooting at. If he does this he will find that the apportionment for postage stamps and paper falls off considerably—and the chances of sale will rise in the same proportion.

The Adventure field is not quite so cluttered yet with new titles, but that makes it all the more advisable for new writers to take a whirl at it. The uptrend for Adventure yarns is just beginning, while Gangster got its initial surge some time ago—albeit it is still climbing. In addition to *Far East Adventure Stories*, which was the first of the new magazines out this fall, other magazines now out in that field are *All-Fiction*, *Oriental Stories*, *Man Stories*, and *Star Magazine*. The first issues of these new magazines are on the stands now, and the beginning writer who intends to cash in on them should pick up copies and read them through thoroughly, before he sends out any manuscripts that he has on hand. Each editor wants a particular type of story and it usually differs from the requirements of the rival editor in the same field. This is the age of specialization, and nowhere is it more apparent than in the pulp-paper magazine field. All stories can be divided into three classes, love, adventure, or mystery-detective; but look at the number of offshoots each class has.

And oddly enough, the Gangster story is not an offshoot from the mystery-detective class. I know most of you will place it there, but its predecessor was old Papa Adventure, and the thing to have in mind when you write such a story is the adventure angle and not the detective angle. There is no great crime to be solved by clever deductive reasoning of Sherlock Holmes type heroes; rather it is the straight out-and-out action story with the hero splattering plenty of blood with fist and gun.

The Gangster field is now approaching its peak, but there is yet time for the new writer to crash in if he will confine his efforts to sharpshooting at particular magazines in the field. Pick out one and go to it. Keep plugging until you hit.

The Far East-Oriental field is the latest outgrowth of the parent adventure story. It is exemplified at present by two magazines, my own *Far East Adventure Stories*, and *Oriental Stories*, published by Farnsworth Wright in Chicago. The field is exactly the same and covers the same territory. Yet, a story that fits *Oriental Stories* occasionally will come a long ways from fitting *Far East*, and the opposite is true also. So far there are but these two in this field, but rumbling rumors are about already. If either one makes a success there are a dozen publishers chaffing at the bit now, ready to plunge in as soon as the final word comes through.

But shooting at the moon won't land checks from either one of the above magazines, nor those that will follow later. The beginner will have to get down to sharpshooting and do so quickly, otherwise he will remain just what he is, an amateur-writer and nothing else.

As for my proving that this method works, I have only to refer you to myself. Less than four years ago I was a beginning writer and I will admit that I did most of my shooting at the moon. When I got down to facts and began sharpshooting, I began to hit and hit regularly, and I have been doing so ever since. Of course the matter of luck entered into it, also. I was fortunate enough to have sense enough to write nothing but Air stories after Lindbergh made his historic hop. But luck is a factor that none of us can control, so we have to work with the idea in mind that there is no such thing. If we are lucky, so much the better. If we are not, well, it just means that we have to keep on plugging until our luck changes, which it is bound to do—in time.

And the fact that I was a beginning writer not so long ago hasn't escaped me yet. I have lots of sympathy for beginners, knowing that the path to success is strewn with thorns. I plucked many out of my own flesh on the way up. To make it easier for the beginning writer to crash in for profits, I have instituted a "New Author's Corner" in *Far East Adventure Stories*, wherein nothing but stories by authors who have never appeared in print before will be published. And what is more, they will be paid good rates on acceptance.

I think that by that I have proved my loyalty to the beginner. Now if the beginner will return the favor and cease shooting at the moon, in the manuscripts he sends in to me and all the other editors in the magazine field, I am sure he will improve his own condition and chances for graduation into the big-money class.

If any of you who have read this article have received anything of benefit from it, don't thank me for it. Thank Mr. Hawkins, the editor of this magazine. He has paid me to write the article, and that is all the thanks I ask from anyone. You will, of course, see from this last statement that I am a cold-blooded writer who writes for profit and nothing else. And that is just what I want you to see and feel. When you get down to doing the same thing yourself, the checks will roll in faster.

Stop shooting at the moon.

Start sharpshooting instead!

[*The Author & Journalist*, January 1931]

Richard A. Martinsen
Executive Editor, *War Stories*, *Sky Riders*, and *Scotland Yard*
Of the Dell publications
Has the honor to present—

What In Thunder *Is* Their Policy?

*A modern one-act drama which, in letter or verbal form,
Has had more performances than "Abie's Irish Rose."*

Richard A. Martinsen

[Dick Martinsen fought in the World War—the "late excitement" as it was fondly remembered then—working his way up from the cavalry to an officer in the infantry. After the war, he earned a degree from Stanford, then went into the newspaper business, finally editing a Santa Barbara newspaper after about five years. He started supplementing his income by selling pulp stories on the side, mostly to Fiction House: *Action Stories*, *True Adventures*, *The Lariat*. When that started to look like a better gig than the newspaper racket, he moved to New York. By early '26, he was employed at Fiction House, editing *North-West Stories*. He resigned in the middle of '27 as managing editor of the chain, and thereafter expanded his freelance markets. He continued to appear in Fiction House pulps, but also became a regular in Fawcett's *Triple-X* and *Battle Stories*. He later returned to editing, at Dell. The timing is uncertain, but his name doesn't emerge as a presence there until after the shakeup that saw Harry Steeger and A.A. Wyn resign from the company (see the Carson Mowre profile preceding "What An Editor Really Thinks"). With that, Martinsen assumed responsibility for *Navy Stories*, *War Novels*, and *War Stories*. *Navy Stories* and *War Novels* were discontinued by the end of the year; *Sky Riders* and *Scotland Yard* were added to his roster. One day, he received a submission for *Scotland Yard* by a young Lester Dent. According to an account in *Writer's Review* (April 1935): "Martinsen wired him back to come to New York if he were making less than a hundred a week and he'd be given a drawing account of five hundred a month and taught to become a writer. Dent quit his job as telegraph operator, came East and within a short time was writing the entire issue of *Scotland Yard* under a dozen pennames." The event can be dated to early '31, when *Scotland Yard* stopped soliciting freelance submissions. It would have been a great deal for the writer and the editor—had it worked. We assume it failed, and perhaps helped sink Martinsen's career with Dell, for within two months, *Sky Riders* had been merged into Mowre's *War Aces*, new hire A.H. Bittner was editing

War Stories, and Martinsen was gone. *Scotland Yard* struggled on for several issues after his departure. Martinsen's name doesn't surface in the pulp field after 1931. The Dell experience may have soured him, or perhaps made him an undesirable hire at another house. Of his five Dell pulps, four failed within short order. (*War Stories*, under Bittner, lasted until the issue of June 1932.) He may simply have been a victim of the collapsing war pulp genre, which left him a military specialist without a seat at the table.]

(*The scene is a woodpulp editorial sanctum, a little affair of glass and beaver-board partitions strangely reminiscent of a glorified cheese-box; one of a row of cubbyholes leading off a long corridor, like a maze of rabbit-warrens.*

The EDITOR, *who resembles one of the five million budding young executives in any great national organization in guise and garb, occupies a swivel-chair in front of a flat-topped desk.*

Upon a plain and uncomfortable straight chair, beside the desk, is seated the WRITER, *who is very probably—YOU.*

The click of typewriters and bee-like hum of the nearby general offices furnishes steady accompaniment for the ensuing dialogue.

Inject the stage-business and pantomime to suit yourself. It's all a matter of individual temperament.)

WRITER: I'd understand your tossing those last three stories back at me if I hadn't sold you. But you took my first yarn right off the bat.

EDITOR: Um-m.

WRITER: And those yarns weren't duds, either. I've already sold one of 'em to *He-Man Tales*.

EDITOR: That's fine. *He-Man Tales* is a good market.

WRITER: Huh?

EDITOR: I said *He-Man Tales* is a first-rate market. Prob'ly pays more than we do. Y'oughta build yourself up there.

WRITER: But you don't get me. I started out to sell you. I don't want to keep shooting away hit-and-miss all the time. I want to get two or three good markets and plug 'em regularly.

EDITOR: That's a good idea, too. The trouble with those last three yarns is that they weren't in line with my policy for *Gallant Stories*.

WRITER: Gee-gosh! Didn't I just tell you I sold one to *He-Man Tales*? Your *Gallant Stories* covers exactly the same field!

EDITOR: True. But my policy differs, just the same. You've proved it by the sale you made.

WRITER: You might as well tell me there's a difference in the policies of *West* and *Lariat*—

EDITOR: There certainly is.
WRITER: Or *Adventure* and *Action Stories*—
EDITOR: Even more decidedly!
WRITER: Or *Love Story* and *Sweetheart*—
EDITOR: Hold your horses a moment. You're getting over my head. One thing at a time. I'll admit I didn't think there was much distinction between heartthrob yarns myself until the other day, when I passed the manuscript of a friend of mine down the line, and found it was too this for *Modern Love*, too that for *Sweetheart*, and too t'other for *Cupid's Diary*. However, I don't profess to know the women's list, so that's out. If you want me to shed a little illumination on the men's books, though, I'll try.
WRITER: Proceed.
EDITOR: To begin with, we must divide the field into its principal elements, to wit: detective, Western, air, war, adventure, and general fiction. There are numerous sub-classifications, but this being a lecture and not a seminar we can't tackle 'em. Now, of the main groups, which d'you want me to vivisect first?
WRITER: Oh, Westerns will do. They've been my meal-ticket so far.
EDITOR: Very well. Remember that many of the things I say will be more or less controversial. No man can discuss such a variety of shops without falling off the boat on a few fine points, unless he's worked in all of 'em. I'm going to talk not as an editor, but as a writer, with about five years and a hundred or so stories head start on you. The editorial experience is thrown in just for good measure. . . .

Four of the leading Westerns should be enough to open your eyes. We'll take *Western Story*, *West*, *Triple-X Western* and *Lariat*. I've sold plenty copy to three of 'em, and know the fourth pretty definitely. Ostensibly any good Western man-tale ought to find a home with any of these four books. But the average wouldn't.

If your hero happened to be an Eastern tenderfoot, or a young mining engineer, or a sourdough, or a town marshal performing in his official bailiwick, he might get by in the first three, but wouldn't find favor with *Lariat*, which wants stories about real cowboys—mostly on the range. *Triple-X* is tending that way again now, too, although perhaps not so emphatically, and even the other books prefer real puncher heroes doling their stuff in the open.
WRITER: Yeah. That's elementary. But—
EDITOR: But we're just beginning. So much for heroes. Now: if the first three paragraphs of your yarn establish your setting—paint an artistic, colorful atmosphere, that's very nice, but it's curtains, so far as *Lariat* is concerned. Ralph Daigh out at *Triple-X* wouldn't like it much, and even Roy Horn's brows, on *West*, would pucker slightly, unless it was very well done indeed. The best bet, then, is to start off at a gallop.

Writer: Yeah. And gallop all the way, what I mean!

Editor: Then don't mean it too strenuously. Because you can't gallop too hard and remain plausible And if you're not doggone plausible from gaff to fantail, *West* and *Western Story* will issue return tickets, while if you're too calmly plausible, *Triple-X* and *Lariat* will have none of you.

I've evolved a two-way target that's been working pretty well for some time. If a yarn is tossed back by *West* as too melodramatic, *Triple-X* usually corrals it, while if *Triple-X's* reaction to a yarn is violently jaundiced, *West* not infrequently picks it up. If both these books jump on a yarn, however, I toss it in the lowest drawer forthwith. There's something radically wrong.

Generally speaking, a yarn that *Triple-X* and *Lariat* will clutch avidly won't sell to *Western Story* or *West*, and vice versa. Yes, speaking *very* generally. For each of these mags has a number of its own peculiar wants and don'ts—*West* a particular lot of 'em. And *Western Story*, f'rinstance, is a deal more addicted to the sentimental side of range life and character than *West*. And *Lariat* wants elementary simplicity. A yarn with the least trace of the supernatural, bogus or real, used as frame-up by the villains or as fact, is *out* for *West*. And *West* isn't keen for railroads in the cow country, and doesn't like Indians, while *Triple-X* doesn't want—

Writer: Whoa! Whoa! Have a heart! Let's change the subject.

Editor: Don't you want to discuss the other Western markets? A Western is a Western, you know.

Writer: I know it *isn't* by now, not being stone-deaf. Let's talk about adventure books.

Editor: All right. There aren't so many of those. Let's see. *Action Stories*, *Adventure*, *Short Stories*, and *All-Fiction* are fair samples. No. Maybe we'd better switch *Short Stories* from adventure to general fiction. Its policy is pretty broad: J.S. Fletcher to H. Bedford-Jones, and most everything in between. We'll substitute Wally Bamber's new *Far East*.

Well, if Jack Kelly and Jack Byrne over at *Action Stories* received all the manuscripts submitted to *Adventure*, they'd turn down 95 percent of 'em. And Proctor, of *Adventure*, would turn down a good fat 93 percent of the stories finding homes at Fiction House. You see, the shops are playing to entirely different galleries—or think they are. *Action Stories* wants high pressure from beginning to end. The hero is welcome to kill fifty villains with ten shots, if the feat is put across convincingly. But no matter how convincing it sounded, or what illusion of reality was achieved, that wouldn't go in *Adventure*. Ten in ten shots would be plenty. *Far East* might conceivably stand fifteen, and *All-Fiction* twenty.

The point is that with *Action*, and in lesser degree with *All-Fiction* and *Far East*, powerful drama and a cogent, compelling story are the thing—the big thing—while with *Adventure* there are numerous other, and scarcely less important considerations. Every hair on the cow's back must not only be carefully tabulated, but in its proper place. *Adventure* is an etching. *Action Stories* is a poster. Each in its way is art.

I've mentioned only basic differences, so far. *Action Stories* wants outdoor adventure. *Adventure* will upon occasion use city stuff, with a detective or mystery slant. *Far East* constrains itself to the geographic area conveyed by its title. *All-Fiction* uses the world for a playground. Carson Mowre has no set formula, but just the same a story has to be mighty virile and move along swiftly to hit him.

Another thing: though most of the "adventure" magazines profess wide range of locales, most of them feature and give most space to a certain type of story in a specific locale. It used to be Westerns. Then the air and Foreign Legion chiseled in for a while, with detective on the side. Now it's largely Western again. And if a writer wants to hit something, it's good sense to shoot at the biggest hole

Adventure yarns are safe and solid stuff. They have an exceptionally wide field, because most of the so-called general fiction books also plunge on them. But there again, nearly each magazine has its pet types and anathemas, its favored treatment, its—

WRITER: Yes, I know. About a thousand things a fellow can't get even by analyzing a copy of the magazine itself. I'm beginning to think it's a miracle if a novice makes a sale.

EDITOR: Strangely enough, it isn't as much of a stunt to sell one or two stories, as it is to get rid of most of your copy when you've won your spurs and are producing regularly. Then the first fine edge of enthusiasm is taken off your stories, and prob'ly off your characters and plots. To make up for that you have to hew right to the line in matters of magazine policy—which is another way of saying salesmanship.

WRITER: Ah, yes. That too has a familiar and bromidic ring. The problem is to find out what these complex and innumerable elements of policy are. We'll skip the detectives—

EDITOR: Oh, sure. A mere bagatelle. There are only thirty-six of 'em.

WRITER: Each differing a shade in type and policies, I presume?

EDITOR: Pretty nearly. There are the inductive reasoning, the two-fisted, the gangster books, the mystery, the pseudo-scientific, the horror—

WRITER: Well, let's skip 'em anyhow. And the air books. And the war books—

EDITOR: There are only two of those left, now. All around war. World War, of course. They're *Battle Stories* and *War Stories*. And it happens that their policies are much the same.

WRITER: Well, thank the Lord for something! Could you elucidate that policy in a nutshell?

EDITOR: Straight action-formula. Start off in high, and keep stepping right along. Land, sea, or air. Locale anywhere, with war background—

WRITER: Entirely too pat. You must have primed for it. Let's get along to the general fiction books. There should be some good markets there.

EDITOR: There are. From the out-and-out woodpulps, like *High Spot, Excitement, Complete,* and *Top-Notch,* to magazines which verge almost on the slicks in policies—and prices, too.

WRITER: As for instance?

EDITOR: *Short Stories* and *Blue Book.* The old *Popular* was the greatest Roman of them all, and still carries along. *Argosy* isn't far behind, either, and *Five-Novels* wants good writing as well as peppy action.

WRITER: This seems to have developed into an enumeration of markets, instead of advice on how to hit 'em. I have a market list.

EDITOR: The best market list in the world is only a catacomb of skeletons. Skeletons measure pretty well to scale, but you can't get the picture of the flesh and blood people from 'em. Ten men may be bank cashiers, yet all differ in temperament, likes and dislikes. Magazines are the same. To learn their individualities you have to know them, and to know them you have to come into personal contact.

WRITER: O Solomon! You were about to propound the policies of the general fiction books, if I recall.

EDITOR: To be sure. Well, the platform of the best ones is the least cut-and-dried in the pulp field. *Short Stories* tends to adventure, and outdoor stories on the whole. The off-trail stories are apt to be the longer length, feature stuff with prominent names to help 'em crash the gate. But Roy Horn will knuckle onto almost any good yarn, so long as it's written from the man-slant, doesn't engender race prejudice, and leaves a pleasant taste.

There's no limit in type save the sky for *Blue Book,* either. Pick up any issue and you'll see a thoroughly balanced ration.

Richards of *Complete Stories* and Laurence of *Top-Notch* are among the other editors who'll tell you they have no formula, and are sincere in it. But you'll find they have their inhibitions, their likes and dislikes, all the same.

WRITER: That's natural, since they're human—as human, at least, as editors ever are.

EDITOR: Horsefeathers! It'd do most of you fellows good to wield the scepter for a while. You'd soon find it was more like a shovel, and that the throne-room in many respects resembled one of Chic Sale's ingenious structures.

Most of the delays, oversights, and slights that irk you are due to the high pressure under which the modern woodpulp editor works. Most of us are in sweat mills, swamped with mechanical routine. We've come to be primarily detail men. The leisure, reflection, and pedagogic mellowness that used to be associated with a literary sanctum are not for us.

If an editor is giving you uniformly quick service, friendly cooperation, and intelligent reactions, you can bet he's an unusually conscientious soul, and is doing a good part of his reading and real thinking o' nights. Otherwise he's slighting some element of his work, doesn't know a good job from a bad one, or doesn't care.

WRITER: Alas! I weep for you. . . . But we were talking magazine policies, I think. Or was the oration complete?

EDITOR: I could keep going all day and not scratch the surface. But it wouldn't help you much. You've got to learn by experience, in writing as in other things. All I can do is get you started working along the right lines intelligently. If I haven't already done that, it's hopeless.

I'm only going to mention one more important and at the same time widely divergent element. That's story length, a matter to which many of you chaps appear to pay no attention at all. Believe me you should. A 6000-word short is good for any magazine anywhere. There are several books which don't mind an extra thousand or so, but there are more which most decidedly do. And if you slop over, when a book specifies a 6000-word limit, you're just building a wall in front of your manuscript. True, a cracking good story will leap any wall. But average copy won't.

WRITER: I've heard of machine-made fiction. Now I realize what the term means. Does every story have to be turned out on a lathe?

EDITOR: No. If you're enough of an artist, you can carry on in your own sweet way. There's always a market for literature, in the old sense. But it isn't the woodpulps.

As for that, there are a few writers in our field who soar above ordinary barriers. Joel Rogers is one. Joel knocks about every rule for the action story into a cocked hat. I don't know whether he's good because he does it, or does it because he's good. He puts in the action when and where he feels like it. But he creates *men*, and rambles along with such excellent feel that the reader will stay with him indefinitely. And so will the editors.

Policies are evolved for the average performer, in pulp-paper fiction as in all else. For him, though, they're ironclad.

WRITER: A pox on the whole system! Why should I invite a brainstorm trying to absorb your confounded foibles? I'll get an agent and let him do the worrying!

EDITOR: Not such a bad idea. However, the best agent in the country can't market an unsalable story. Unless you study your field, and conform to its policies, you are placing your agent under an impossible handicap. If he's a good man he'll shoot your stories back at you as fast as an editor. Your chief benefit will be his coaching, and that's fair enough, provided you are willing to pay for it.

Despite his best endeavors, the average agent in our field already suffers from surplus of aimlessly written stories, judging by what flows over my desk.

The novitiate feels he's achieved quite a feat merely in getting a complete story out of his system. That's only natural. And it isn't until the glow of the first few birth-throes wears off, and the yarns come trotting home again, that he finds his sea legs and starts really cleaving to a given line.

The fault of overrunning word lengths is also usually associated with the fiction tyro. Most of the 8000 or 9000-word manuscripts I see are 6000-word stories lacking crispness and proper condensation.

The 10,000 to 12,000-word story is the worst of all, as a sales prospect. It falls midway between short story and novelette length, and is available for very few magazines.

Writer: Dear me. You chaps appear to dictate length, treatment, types, beginnings and endings. It's a wonder you don't standardize plots, and make an end of it.

Editor: They're already standardized. Human reactions haven't changed much in the last two thousand years.

Writer: A lot you care about human reactions! Action is your only battle-cry.

Editor: Why not? A real action plot is good for any magazine.

Writer: In the pulp-paper field, you mean.

Editor: Every field. The way you put it over is the determining factor. It's your style and presentation that align a story with a definite type of book. A versatile writer could do the same plot three different ways and sell it to three different kinds of magazines.

Writer: Credible in theory, but I'd like to see someone do it.

Editor: I have.

Writer: No foolin'? What was your plot?

Editor: Never mind. There are plenty. I'll outline another: a young Westerner comes riding over the hill. He's an outlaw, with a posse in pursuit. He evades the law temporarily, however, and applies for a ranch job in another county. It seems to the rancher's sweet and innocent little daughter that Prince Charming has arrived. Her illusion impels the outlaw to play the role, which grows so natural that when a gang of rustlers spots him and promptly arranges a raid, he can't bring himself to participate. In fact, he warns the rustlers off. However, they think he's got a joker up his sleeve, and carry on despite him. The bad-good man is now in a tight spot. His code forbids squealing, and yet he can't kill the faith of the girl. Hence he decides upon voluntary suicide, going out to stop the raid single-handed. There's a whale of a scrap, and the good-bad man is surrounded. As the outlaws close in to finish him off, however, the law appears headed by the ranch punchers and the girl's father. They were privy to developments. Even the girl had known the good-bad man was an outlaw. In fact, the local sheriff had promised the girl's father that if the ex-outlaw stood this test, he'd help secure a pardon. . . .

WRITER: And what are the magazines you'd pick for that old hack?

EDITOR: It'd go most anywhere, properly dressed. However, let's pick three books as far apart as the poles. How about *The Saturday Evening Post*, a woman's magazine—say the love magazine put out for Woolworth's by the Tower Publications—and, oh, *Action Stories*.

WRITER: You couldn't make it. Not enough girl for the love book, and too much of her for *Action*.

EDITOR: Wrong. It all depends on how the love element is handled. For the *Post* we tell the story abstractly, and let it develop normally. For *Action* we tell the story through male eyes, crowd in the dramatic tension and high-pressure action, and suppress the girl to a pastel of motivation. For the love book we stick to the girl, and key down on the gore.

WRITER: I'd certainly like to see the three complete manuscripts!

EDITOR: This is a chat, not a short-story course, so I'll not accommodate. However, you don't need the entire stories. The opening paragraphs in each case will give you the idea. Give me a few minutes and I'll knock those out for you.

WRITER: Good. I'll go outside and read a paper until you call.

(Fifteen minutes later)

EDITOR: All right. Here you are. This one's the *Post* opening.
WRITER (reads):

> There was a sense of unreality about the scene. The serried walls of granite thrust their heads into the sky like brooding sentinels. Even the brilliant sun drenched the place with garish color instead of warmth. It was as though Nature had caught its breath, so deep was the hush which lay upon this western world, so motionless . . . as vivid, but as empty as an abandoned stage.
>
> Yet the illusion of desolation was not long sustained. From far in the distance came a sharp crackle, like the breaking of dry sticks. A moment later, with a silvery jingle and muffled creaking, a horse and rider appeared on a rocky knoll to the right of the winding trail. The skyline etched the rider in sharp profile as he twisted in his saddle to peer keenly behind him . . . a lean face. . . .

EDITOR: Now try the heartthrob.
WRITER (reads):

> With a little sigh Janet watched the rabbit pop under a clump of

sage. A half-wistful smile quirked the corners of her intriguing lips. Alas, even Mr. Bunny Cottontail had more pressing concerns in life than a mere girl!

She raised herself to an elbow. Her eyes fastened dreamily upon the nearby hilltop, with the dome of heaven painted above it in vast azure masterstrokes. It was a panorama of romance, an exalting blue and golden fairyland. Yet something was lacking.... It came to Janet with another little sigh. She was lonely.

And then—

EDITOR: Then two shots off stage, and enter Prince Charming.

WRITER: But I say: the scene was completely empty in the *Post* opening. No girl around, or anything.

EDITOR: Different theater, different stage. Same aim, though. We're introducing the hero as he rides over the hill. Now let's get him into the *Action* yarn.

WRITER (reads):

As startling, as harrowing as the crack of doom were the two shots which crashed along the canyon walls, tossed and retossed like the growls of a Satanic laughter.

As though the tumult had been a signal, a horseman rocketed over the skyline.

Doom's messenger—a reckless human thunderbolt pressing close to the saddle, his lean face set and grim, eyes glittering with a danger flame, the rider drove along. Once he twisted to look behind him, and his lips twitched scornfully....

EDITOR: And there you are.

WRITER: You've taken unfair advantage again, though. You've speeded up your rider as well as your style. He was just loafing along in the *Post* opening.

EDITOR: Very well. Let him loaf, and harp on his contemptuous laugh as he turns to peer behind him. What I attempted to show primarily was the necessary changes in viewpoint as well as style. But mark one thing. The action opening might conceivably get by in the *Post*—it'd have to be considerably less crude than this one, of course—but the *Post* opening would definitely kill the yarn for *Action Stories*. Nine chances in ten the readers would never look beyond it.

WRITER: Ergo, stick by the action opening, eh?

EDITOR: That's it. From the standpoint of psychology on shop readers, the first two or three paragraphs are the most important in your story. Bob Hardy or Rusty White—anyway, one of our leading agents—recently told me he'd been trying to impress that fact on his writers for the last three years, and most of 'em haven't learned it yet.

WRITER: Well, I have. And quite a few other things, for which I'm duly grateful.

EDITOR: All right. Come on, then. It's up to you to buy the drinks.

[*Writer's 1931 Year Book*]

What an Editor Really Thinks
Carson Mowre

[Very little of a biographical nature is known of Carson W. Mowre. He was a Naval aviator in the Great War, and a horseman. That's it and that's not much, but both attributes would figure in his pulp career. Current records show him entering the scene in May 1928 with stories in the Fiction House pulps *Action Stories*, *Lariat Story*, and *Wings*. He was already, or became, a Fiction House editor. By the end of summer, 1929, he had joined Dell Publishing. His first assignment was *War Novels*, taking over the title from Eugene A. Clancy. In the September '29 *Author & Journalist*, Harold Hersey announced a new hybrid: *Love and War Stories*. A month later, a similar announcement came from Dell: Mowre would launch a new title to be called *War Romances*, which fit with their *War Birds/War Novels/War Stories* triumvirate. Another month later, he added a new pulp to his responsibilities, *Western Romances*, and began development of a sports pulp. In due course, *Love and War Stories* came and went in Hersey-fashion: it lasted an issue. That may have dimmed Dell's ardor for their own version, because the *War Romances* concept was killed soon thereafter. The sports mag was postponed as well and, in fact, never appeared. In mid-'30, a round of musical chairs among pulp editors sent long-lasting shock waves through the industry. Harry Steeger, Mowre's colleague, and the editor of *War Birds*, among others, quit Dell to join forces with Harold Goldsmith, managing editor of Magazine Publishers, to form a new and significant company, Popular Publications. Another Dell editor, A.A. Wyn, took Goldsmith's job, eventually remaking the company into the more familiar Ace Group. The shakeup cleared the way for Mowre to become managing editor of all the Dell pulps, although the timing is uncertain. Among the Dell staff, Richard A. Martinsen took over editing *War Novels*. That would have left Mowre with only *Western Romances*, but he started another new magazine, *War Aces*, in essence, a revamped *War Romances*. Dell bucked conventional wisdom in starting a new Great War pulp at the time; they were on the downslide. In recognition, Mowre aimed to specialize in "different" air-war stories, which included stories from the German point of view. The acclaimed film *All Quiet on the Western Front*, a story from the German side, premiered in April 1930, and Dell's slant may not have been a coincidence. Like other publishers, Dell continued to experiment with new titles, and even 5¢ pulps (*All Detective*, *All Western*, for a time). Editorship continued to shift among the staff occasionally. At the start of 1936, Mowre left Dell to start some new venture. He reappeared in the pulps as an author soon after, and as late as 1938, air-war and western. After that, his trail goes cold. :: That's the timeline. As an editor, Mowre regarded himself an "entertainment expert." He had a reputation for demanding strong material, e.g. "Heroes must be strongly characterized and big enough so that the reader can crawl into the said hero's skin, see the story through his senses." Arthur J. Burks had the habit of thinking up an intriguing title, then making up the rest on the fly. "If I have a story when I finish, I sell it to Carson W. Mowre. . . . If I don't have a story, I try to sell it somewhere else." Mowre mastered the sharpened tongue, as will be obvious from the below article. In a letter to *Writer's Digest* (reprinted in *Pulp Fictioneers*), he referred to his customers, the pulp readers, as "morons." Veteran fictioneer Allan Bosworth wrote: "Carson Mowre . . . used to write me very salty letters, giving me hell when the yarns fell below par." Here is a sampling of Mowre's savory solicitations: "Our magazine is making no effort to appeal to Easterners who get a vicarious thrill out of much lead-slinging, rustling, etc. It is making its appeal direct to the Westerner, and people who have lived in the West. So many of the so-called Western books have nauseated real Westerners that we are trying to give them something different to read. . . . We want to portray a true picture of the West with all its color and glamour, not a ribbon clerk's version of an hombre with a Colt in each hand, killing 47 sheriffs, not to mention 16 U.S. marshals and countless rangers." "The simpering, gushy type of fiction is not wanted and sex will not be the kind that rears an ugly head." *All Detective* wants "blood, thunder, menace and murder." "Just forget all about the women in the world when you're writing that good atmospheric Western for Dell." Dell made sport of Mowre one Christmas by sending out cards showing him killing Santa Claus.]

WHEN THE EDITOR OF THIS ANNUAL suggested that an article telling his readers just what the editor of a large publishing house thought about the new writer, he struck a theme that is packed with dynamite. Few new writers, or, rather, I should say, few new aspirants to be writers, ever know exactly what the editor thinks about their work. Why should they when that convenient little device, the rejection slip, is so handy?

That sounds more brutal than it really is, but no editor has the time to write a criticism on stories that are rejected, unless, of course, he thinks he sees a budding genius on those typewritten pages. The tyro merely has the consolation of a diplomatically worded little slip that informs him of the editor's inability to use the story. If the young author has the courage of his convictions he keeps on sending it out and, quite likely, gathers a sizable flock of those irritable little slips.

And thereby hangs the gist of this article: the average editor really thinks that most of the beginners in the writing profession would make highly proficient street car conductors. Deep down in him, to elaborate, the average editor would like to devise a plan whereby he could collect a bounty on their scalps.

That statement has, no doubt, taken the wind out of your sails and left you either grimacing with the suppressed desire to commit mayhem or has led you to believe that this will be a frank discussion of the new writers' problems. And it is to be just that.

Why, you ask, do editors regard the newcomer with such downright scowls? Didn't the best known writers today have to write their first stories? Weren't their stories as bad as my beginning efforts? Then what right have you to explode such a bombshell among us? Bah! Your liver is tinctured with venom and your mother's aunt had hangnails. You'd like to be another Mencken.

The answer to that fancied outburst is simple.

Every well-known writer had to write his first story; obviously. And many of those first efforts were probably worse than yours. And I have a right to explode such a bombshell because it is true—painfully so. Let us look over the situation and see what basis of truth there is to the above statements and if any normal editor has a right to entertain such monstrous thoughts about the newcomer.

In the United States alone there are roughly 120 million people. Of that number, it is a known fact that several hundred thousand people are writing or have tried their hand at it. Quite a crowd, isn't it? But the question arises, what fitness have all these people that qualifies them to become writers or even gives them the hope that they will someday become great literary lights? In ninety percent of the cases they have exactly none.

It is that ninety percent of that multitude that gives the average editor his or her feeling of disgust. Immediately some of my readers will cite cases of acquaintances who have sold their first story, or of people who became famous as literary geniuses at twenty. True—but those are rare. And check up those geniuses who achieved fame at twenty. Where are they today? Gone as quickly as they blazed across the literary firmament. Practically every writer of distinction today has put in long hard years of study and effort and writing and writing to get where he is. He has earned that success. What, then, gives all these scribblers the idea that, though other fields of endeavor take years of preparation, all you need to become a writer is paper and pencil or a secondhand, broken-down typewriter?

The main reason for this huge daily migration of unfit manuscripts to editorial sanctums is a product of our modern luxury. The people of this country have the time and the means to read and buy the products of hundreds of publishers. America has become magazine conscious. Daily on newsstands thousands of periodicals are on display. Is it any wonder that this great army of would-be writers labor under the delusion that they, too, can write?

We are not concerned with setting the blame for this flood of literature and so-called literature. Suffice it to say that when a reading public has demonstrated that they will buy, there will be publishers to print. But therein lies the reason for this great myth that *anybody can write*. Such a display of the finished products of writers has built up that roseate illusion that writing is a gold mine—that in no time you can become famous.

Nothing is further from the truth! To become successful even in a minor way takes at least *five* years of painstaking, heartbreaking labor and study, and ten years' apprenticeship has been served by many.

Of the better class of magazines dealing in fiction a certain little group of writers, no more than three hundred in number, write ninety percent of the fiction. Of the second class of the magazines, known as the "pulps," the situation is much the same, while that writing group may exceed the other by two hundred writers. What, then, becomes of those other thousands and thousands of writers who are daily scribbling away? They are exactly where they belong in the writing profession—nowhere.

A banker who has taken twenty years of work and study to fit him for the position he now holds, fondly coddles the idea that he is fitted to write. He writes what he considers to be the perfect story and sends it out to set the world afire. He has not the acumen to know that it will take a corresponding number of years of work and study to fit him to become a successful writer as it did to become a banker. And yet he has the temerity to write an editor a sharp letter telling him he doesn't know his business when that pert little rejection slip drops out on his desk.

To state it in blunt facts, no profession, art or trade, pins the accolade of success on its workers without study and effort of the hardest kind, least of all writing. Why, even a ditch digger who has had to devote a modicum of time and effort to learn how to do his work efficiently, thinks because he has had certain experiences that he can write them down and become a literary success. Just another wisp of that popular myth.

A doctor will spend seven years in college preparing himself for the day when he can hang out his shingle, and another five years of practice before he can count himself a success, and yet some callow youth just out of high school will imagine because he has written an essay or composition that his instructor praised, that he is to become another Kipling immediately. He has nothing to say. He is undeveloped. But nevertheless he will continue to write amateurish piffle and bombard editors with it.

There is no royal road to royalties or editorial checks without study and effort. Possibly a few facts taken from the everyday routine of a large publishing house will illustrate the truth of these statements more plainly.

Each morning the mailman dumps sacks of manuscripts on the readers' desks. Quite probably in that first mail there will be two thousand. Of those two thousand not over one hundred will be given serious consideration. The others are sent back. Upon rereading that one hundred will be weeded out to fifty or less. Those fifty are passed on to the editors of the various magazines. Of those fifty the editor might probably buy two, or in extreme cases three.

Quite a low percentage. What of those other hundreds—why haven't they "clicked"? They have failed for many reasons. Many of them had been sent haphazardly in hopes of a sale—they were no more suited to the type of magazine they were sent to than wings were to Mephistopheles. Others were simply and rankly amateurish. The large majority of them showed that their authors knew nothing whatever about the trade they were trying to make a success at. Again, let me say that it is that large majority which has plainly demonstrated its unfitness that gives the newcomer his initial black eye with editors.

I might quote another example of the strength of this mythical genii who give this magic power to write by a mere touch.

Just a day or so ago a truck driver who delivers books to our warehouse came boldly into my office and dropped a large, voluminous manuscript on my desk. Even before his words were out I recognized the symptoms. He had the great American novel there.

"Howdy, Chief. Will youse take a look at this story? I been readin' them magazines you print and I tells the goil friend I kin do as good any day."

Possibly you can imagine what the story was like. It started with a capital letter and ended with a period. That lad is going to be very indignant when I hand it back to him and tell him to stick to trucks. He'll have to have at least fourteen other editors tell him the same thing before he gets the virus out of his system.

You say that example doesn't apply to a well-educated man who is a great deal more fitted by reason of his education to write. It fits all classes of people who have not put in their period of apprenticeship. It is possible that a college graduate can know less about writing than a truck driver.

To further tear down the structure of the colossal myth that has done so much harm, let us look into the writing life of a few authors whose success is known to all. Kipling wrote hundreds of stories before his *Plain Tales From the Hills* established him in the literary world. He worked and studied and wrote and learned by writing. His was no overnight success. Mark Twain didn't establish his fame as a humorist by writing a few yarns and then waiting for the "success wreath" to fall on his shoulders. He worked for it and when it came after those hard years he was ready and had earned it.

Of the present-day popular writers who enjoy "big names" the same thing holds true. Ben Ames Williams wrote over one hundred stories before he ever sold one. Jim Tully was not the flash across the literary horizon he seemed to be; he wrote much before he ever interested an editor in his work. I could cite hundreds of cases of the best known writers and it would all sound as if it were cut from the same mold.

More questions arise. If, the beginning writer asks, I have the determination and the desire to undergo this period of apprenticeship and am serious in wanting to devote my life to writing, how do I know whether I am writing acceptable material without sending it out to the editors? How did all the writers, who now have made their name, find out whether they could sell their stories without sending them to the different magazines? And if I do this, how do I lift myself from this odious class of misfits? It seems to me you contradict yourself when you say that we must write and write and learn from writing without getting either the benefit of a criticism or a rejection slip.

We'll approach those questions in the sequence which a writer should follow in learning his trade. A doctor wouldn't attempt an operation without having spent considerable time in the study of anatomy. A writer should not, if he ever expects to create anything enduring, attempt to write without the slightest knowledge of plot construction, characterization or a sense of dramatic values. Naturally enough, this knowledge does not drop full-blown into the head of the embryo writer. It is acquired by study in schools or universities, and, if that is not possible to the new writer, by an exhaustive study of textbooks that are available to all. While studying he should be writing constantly. All the study and instruction in the world will not give you the ability to write if you do not learn by doing. I strongly advise the man or woman whose desire it is to become a successful writer to spend at least two years at this sort of study. And under no circumstances should you start bombarding editors with your material during that period of learning, unless, of course, some competent critic has indicated to you that your material is worthy of publication.

Most of our present-day group of writers who enjoy a deserved popularity have followed just such a course. Many of them studied at universities or learned in the school of hard knocks. Many of them came from the newspaper field, but there isn't one in a thousand who arrived overnight as many would have us believe. Many of these people were fortunate enough to have the acquaintance of certain editors who helped them along and gave them friendly tips on what was wrong with their material. Unless you have some entree like this and are sending your stories unsolicited through the mails as you learn, you may expect, unless you show that germ of ability that every editor is on the lookout for, to gather many, oh many, more rejection slips.

To answer the question that inspired this article: How do I lift myself from that multitude of writers who stand little or no chance for publication? Four simple sentences should answer that.

First, assure yourself that you have the intestinal fortitude to withstand that grueling period of disappointment and work, and still want to continue. Second, determine whether you have something to say that will make other people want to read what you write—commonly known as ability. Third, do not attempt to write about circumstances, conditions, locales or people with whom you are not familiar. Fourth, by no means send your material the rounds of the publishers until you, yourself, are convinced that you have a story that will appeal, or more sane, that some competent authority has passed on.

Those four sentences could be amplified into all the rules to be found in textbooks, but they are basic. Unless you adhere to them, or are that rarity, genius, you can expect no success in that easiest of all endeavors, writing.

To be a successful author is one of the most graceful of existences. Its remuneration is high and it offers more advantages than many other fields. It is just what many of us picture in our dreams—the ideal way to live and work—but it does not come overnight and it is not gotten without some of the hardest and most discouraging work possible to imagine. And once at that dizzy pinnacle, that position is not maintained by indolence—it means still more work. The climb is a hard one, but if you are fitted for it, the view at the top cannot be excelled.

[*The Author & Journalist*, October 1931]

Trained Seals
Freeman H. Hubbard

[A hobo could have baked his beans off the steam that comes out of Hubbard's ears here. This is a particularly specialized article, addressing the needs of *Railroad Man's Magazine*, but it's also an efficient summary of an editor's frustrations. You can tell he's mad, right down to the last sentence with its delectable dig about the cost of rejection slips. :: This article wasn't the only time Hubbard laid down the law. He frequently railed—forgive the pun—in print about the things he *didn't* want from freelancers: ". . . holdups, boxcar robberies, gunplay, runaway trains, wrecks, near-wrecks, fights in engine cabs, love affairs between railroad men and waitresses, engineers who are 'yellow' but snap out of it later, silk specials that make fast runs in spite of difficulties, forest fires, floods, landslides, villains dynamiting tunnels or bridges, spotters, snowbound trains . . ." "We do not have time to read sophomoric fiction from authors whose style is too trite to sell anywhere else. We do not have time to conduct a correspondence school in 'how to write.' We do not have time to do work that should be done by professional literary critics. If a story really shows promise we'll give plenty of sympathetic editorial cooperation. But Heaven deliver us from the kind of dull, hackneyed, wooden, conventional, journalistic junk that is turned out by the average amateur who never sees below the surface of life—green schoolboys or thick-witted adults who should be plowing lawns or adding up columns of figures." :: Freeman Henry Hubbard (1894-1981) spent a career in pulps and books doing little else than indulging his love of railways. In his own words, the roots ran deep: "My interest in railroad lore dates back to the period before I could talk. My father was a railroad man with a yen for storytelling; my earliest recollections center around the yarns he spun of snowbound trains, fast runs, head-on wrecks, roundhouse cats, track-walking spooks, express bandits, and runaway freight cars." (Sounds like dad would have had difficulty cracking son's magazine.) "Dad worked for the Pennsy and I traveled all over the country and through Canada on his passes. I visited railroad offices, shops, and roundhouses from which the public is usually kept out. I met trainmen and their families, became acquainted with their way of life, and learned their colorful lingo. I rode in engine cabs, cabooses, even a section car. I snapped photographs of locomotives and founded the Railroad Camera Club. I clipped train pictures from magazines and pasted them in scrapbooks. I began collecting a railroad library." Despite never going to college, Hubbard eventually hired on with The Frank A. Munsey Company. It's unclear when he started, but in late '29, Hubbard was an associate editor on the revived title *All-Story*, which was a love pulp, unlike the general fiction magazine of 1905-20. In early 1930, he shifted to the identical position with *Argosy*. In July '29, a fateful event occurred. One William Edward Hayes, another railroad specialist, announced a new line of fiction magazines, its initial title to be, simply, *Railroad*, inspired by Munsey's old *Railroad Man's Magazine*, which had merged with *Argosy* in 1919 as its path to extinction. The Munsey company reacted quickly to Hayes' announcement, taking over his magazine and rechristening it with the old title. With the issue of December '29, *Railroad Man's Magazine* returned to the newsstands—with William Edward Hayes as editor, presumably part of the price Munsey paid for *Railroad*. The event was a godsend for Hubbard. He was editor by July '30. Hayes continued to appear in the magazine—as an author—and, in fact, started placing railroad fiction in *The Saturday Evening Post*, later broadening his markets to mystery, sports, and adventure pulps. But Hubbard had his dream job: "I could not get over the fact that the company paid me during all those years for having fun, for doing the very kind of work I would have been glad to do free of charge if I had been financially independent." The pulp changed title to *Railroad Stories* in 1932, then to *Railroad Magazine* in 1937, when it was felt that fiction was no longer integral to the magazine's success. In late '42, Popular Publications bought out the Munsey chain, keeping five titles active, *Railroad Magazine* among them. Hubbard's associate, Henry B. Comstock, took charge of the magazine while Hubbard became "research editor" for all of Popular. Hubbard continued a successful writing career, selling non-fiction railroad stories to a variety of pulps. Over time, he expanded his markets to men's slicks like *Adventure* and *True*; railroad industry publications; *Popular Science*, *Popular Mechanics*; and even adapted some of his articles for youth magazines like *Jack and Jill*. He also produced books of railroad history, lore, and fiction anthologies. One hit book, *Railroad Avenue, Great Stories and Legends of American Railroading* (Whittlesey House, 1945), was adapted for the radio program *Cavalcade of America*, and condensed in *Liberty*. On the basis of this success, Hubbard left Popular in 1946 for a freelancing career, which he described as "alternately tough and rewarding." Ultimately, "tough" seems to have trumped "rewarding," for Hubbard returned to editing *Railroad Magazine* around 1954, a job he held into the late '60s.]

EVEN AN EDITORIAL MILL HAS ITS RESTRICTIONS. An editor must be diplomatic. He dare not tell would-be contributors what he actually thinks of them for flooding him with manuscripts which a schoolboy could tell were inappropriate.

Sometimes the editor expresses his despair in an ironical letter—which goes over the head of the would-be contributor. I had one such experience when an author, a newspaper reporter, mistook the satire for lavish praise and quoted me to that effect in the paper he worked for!

I know of a case in which an agent submitted a manuscript which, to put it mildly, was extremely unsuitable, and accompanied it with a form letter saying that the story had been selected carefully with a view to the needs of that particular magazine. Well, the editor pointed out tactfully to the agent why the manuscript had *not* been chosen for that magazine, whereupon the agent wrote back an indignant reply—not to the editor, but to the publisher—an action which greatly endeared him to members of the editorial staff!

Because of these and similar incidents, an editor usually masks his real feelings behind a formal rejection slip and rarely lets off steam except in a publication like THE AUTHOR & JOURNALIST. And, in some publishing houses, if he wants appropriate material he assigns a topic to one of his trained seals.*

Outside of downright crudity in style and trite ideas, the commonest reason for rejection of manuscripts is the fact that free-lance writers by the carload attempt to contribute to periodicals they have never seen or at best have only glanced through occasionally. No wonder the number of trained seals is said to be increasing.

Now, I have done quite a bit of freelancing myself, and I realize that an author's funds for buying magazines are limited. Nevertheless, in the face of crowded markets, it is absolutely necessary for him to be familiar with the field he hopes to cover. An editor can detect very quickly whether or not a manuscript has been sent to him on a blind chance.

I have never been able to understand why thousands of writers are so thickheaded as to shoot in the dark, in the vague hope that they may hit some mark. If only they could realize how easy it is to study a magazine carefully and win the editor's undying gratitude by sending him the type of material for which he is hungering and thirsting! But the worst fool of all is, I think, the fellow who has made a study of the magazine but still persists in submitting inappropriate material, on the assumption that the editor doesn't know his business and should be "educated."

Railroad Man's Magazine, for instance, receives a very large amount of inappropriate material—manuscripts which would not have been sent to us if the authors had made a halfway decent effort to discover what type of publication this is.

Railroad Man's is edited "For the Railroad Man and the Railroad Fan"— *not* from the viewpoint of corporation management or the traveling public. Another of our slogans is "The Human Side of Railroading."

And yet every day's mail brings its load of manuscripts that are dull and technical, or vaguely sermonizing on the advisability of the general public supporting the railroad industry, or describing the scenic beauties of some tour, or rehashing material picked out of the railroad company magazines, or filled with propaganda of one kind or another, or dealing with subjects only remotely related to railroading.

Getting back to the railroad company magazines: Virtually all of them come regularly to our office; so do the various brotherhood organs. Authors only waste their time when they dig material from those sources and submit it

---

* Journalese for "staff writers."

to us. Plenty of them do it, too. I wonder if they think we don't know it.

And poetry! We have appealed repeatedly for good, realistic railroad verse, and a lot of half-baked rhymsters delude us with stuff written from the viewpoint of the traveling public.

We get plenty of sugar-coated rhymes about the brave engineer, or the view from the window of a day coach, or the shining steel rails that link one town to another and make neighbors of us all. But very little about drag freight, or the smoky end, or the rivalry between railroad men in various branches of service, or other things near and dear to the man in overalls.

Our readers like plenty of sentiment in their verse, but it must smack of the iron road. Not saccharine idealism written by versifiers who don't know the difference between a mudhop and a brass hat.

Speaking of railroad slang: We published a rather lengthy vocabulary in our June 1930 issue. Ever since that time, we have gotten many good laughs out of amateurish writers (and some successful professionals) who included that lingo in their stories, articles, verse and fillers, without using it properly. They try to fool us with a sprinkling of words and phrases of railroad slang unaccompanied by any real knowledge of railroading.

For instance, a story on my desk right now mentions " 'Tallowpot' Jones, hogger on the crack limited." A "tallowpot" happens to be a fireman, whereas a "hogger" is an engineer, but details like that apparently mean nothing at all to the author.

It is harder for a camel to go through a needle's eye, as the saying runs, than for a non-railroader to write a saleable manuscript for *Railroad Man's Magazine*. We certainly are biased in favor of authors with actual railroad experience, or who at least are members of the immediate families of railroad men.

If you, dear reader, have never done actual railroad work nor associated with railroaders, do not send us manuscripts of any kind. We'd like to save overhead expense on the printing of rejection slips, to say nothing of editorial time and eyesight.

[*The Author & Journalist*, April 1942]

On Relations With Editors
Ray Palmer

[Several science fiction fans graduated into writing and then editing, among them Charles D. Hornig and Robert A.W. Lowndes. Perhaps the best known, because of his varied and colorful career, was Raymond Arthur Palmer (1910-77). He published an early science fiction fanzine, *The Comet*, in 1930. His first professional appearance was "The Time Ray of Jandra" in the June 1930 *Wonder Stories*. Through the decade, he continued to appear in both fanzines and pulps. In early '38, Teck Publications, New Jersey, sold its drab incarnation of *Amazing Stories* to a Chicago firm, the Ziff-Davis Publishing Company. It was ZD's entry into the pulps. Palmer, who lived in Milwaukee, was hired as editor to replace T. O'Conor Sloane. Palmer found himself in charge of the magazine that had meant so much to him as a teenager, when its creator, Hugo Gernsback, published it. Within a year, ZD's polished management and Palmer's knowledgeable editorship turned the pulp from an underperformer into a winner. A companion magazine, *Fantastic Adventures*, was added in 1939. As Ziff-Davis continued to add new pulps to their chain, Palmer's empire, as managing editor, grew. Palmer incited controversy when he published Richard Shaver's pseudoscientific "I Remember Lemuria!" in *Amazing* (March '45). Was it true? Did it belong in a science fiction pulp? As science fiction author Margaret St. Clair wrote (with some exaggeration) in *Writer's Digest* (July '47): "Lately the Ziff-Davis *Amazing Stories* has split science fiction fandom wide-open with the curious 'Shaver Mystery' series of stories about some beings known as 'deroes.' I do not wish to embroil myself in this controversy, and shall only say that I wish Mr. Palmer would dump the whole thing in the bay and go back to presenting his readers with a title page on which five or six names of authors occur, instead of only one, that of Mr. Shaver. We all have to eat." The complaints were to no avail. As long as he remained editor, Palmer continued to publish Shaver's curiosities in *Amazing* and *Fantastic*. In 1948, outside of ZD, Palmer started *Fate* magazine with a first issue (Spring '48) sporting a vision of flying saucers. Palmer had found the successor to the Shaver Mystery and was one of the people most responsible for promoting saucer mania. He resigned ZD after 1949 to devote himself to *Fate*, and a variety of other magazines, fictional or otherwise, which he created.]

HAVING SENT IN A MANUSCRIPT, don't get impatient and write the editor demanding to know what's become of it. If you haven't a report in a reasonable time, just drop him a postal card inquiring if the yarn has been received. Sometimes a manuscript does go astray, and the editor appreciates knowing it, so he can put a tracer on it.

Ziff-Davis has a hidebound rule about service. All manuscripts are either

Ray Palmer

read and accepted, or rejected, or reported on within a few days after they are received. If neither of these things happens, there exists an extraordinary condition: the author will get a letter soon explaining it. Perhaps a new magazine is being launched, or the editor is out of town, or he's celebrating his birthday. Whatever the particular situation, take the matter up with the editor, thrash it out with him, before telling the world the publisher's service is rotten!

Don't be a *detective!* Don't place the tenth page upside down, or put a drop of glue between pages, so you can check up on the editor to see if he *really* has read your manuscript. An editor is pretty egotistic when it comes to his integrity. If he thinks you doubt it, he *might* just slap your manuscript into the envelope and send it back saying, "Why don't you nail it together and bury it in a time capsule?"

Don't worry about the editor stealing your idea. And even if it looks like it, don't raise a howl. A certain author did that recently, saying we'd lifted his idea, and not only that, whole passages, word for word, from a manuscript he'd recently submitted. Wonderful! The manuscript we published had been purchased sixteen months before his came in. His complaint looked pretty silly, and tagged him as a crank whom we don't encourage to submit to us. His name on an envelope is enough to start it back unopened.

Get this: The editor needs you. He's glad you're around. And he'll eat out of your hand if you know how to handle him.

If, by any chance, you can call on the editor, fine. But once a manuscript is in his hands, try not to call on him every other day, or keep dropping in. Especially if he's spent hours helping you with the plot previously. And if he should turn it down, even then, don't gripe. It's just possible *you* missed the boat. Try again.

Most writers like an editor to tell them what's wrong when a story is rejected. Most editors like to comply, but won't because if they dare tell the writer the fault, the writer "fixes" the story up with a flourish and slaps the same manuscript down on the editorial desk with a "now you've got to take it" complex. And the revised story may be worse than the last. If an editor *wants* a story revised, he'll ask you to do it.

If the editor notifies the A&J that he needs manuscripts of a certain type, don't rush him everything in your trunk, stuff that is only remotely related to what he wants, or not related at all. The slant on a new book is even more important. An editor will take the time to tell you what he wants, if you query him.

If he writes you directly, saying "need detective manuscripts," send him some. But if they fail to sell, don't hit the ceiling. He hasn't "ordered" anything from you. He's just put you on his list of "possibles." Even if you have a *name*, you may send a lemon. But if you play ball with him, you're liable to find that in the end, you are a sort of teacher's pet.

Don't get the idea that the editor has "favorites." The guy who sells him a raft of stuff is the guy who started where you are, and used his head, patience, and typewriter to good advantage.

If you write articles, remember that an illustrated article is more likely to cop a check than one not illustrated. Clear, glossy photographs are preferred. It you're not a competent photographer, team up with a freelancer when submitting material. Pencil sketches, in some instances, can be developed into polished drawings by the publisher's art department.

Ghost-written articles are good because they carry an authentic smack, but be sure to get the approval of the man whose byline you want to use.

Never be windy in pulp fiction or articles. Tell your story, and get it over with.

Even a beginner knows a neat manuscript makes a good impression. Buy a new ribbon once in a while, use paper that doesn't blot or tear under an editor's pen, and don't use odd sizes, or onion-skin, or expensive bond.

Aim at your readers, the American people. Give your manuscript firing power. And let's see your work on the desk—soon!

[*Writer's Digest*, March 1944]

Mission To Manhattan
H. Wolff Salz

[H. Wolff Salz mentions the paper shortage. During WWII, publishers were rationed paper based on prewar usage. Pulps shrank in size, some to a mere 80 pages. They contained less fiction, although some of the shortfall was made up by shrinking typefaces. There was also a "writer shortage" with much of the talent serving in the same conflict that drew away the lumber and paper mill workers. Pulp publishers were forced to accept lower-quality fiction and edit it to their standards—or close enough. But this problem was a short-term benefit to the new writers trying to break in. Salz appears to be one of this breed. His publication record starts in 1943. For the next two years he made a number of appearances in *10-Story Detective, Mammoth Detective, Popular Detective*, and others. After '45, nothing. It may be an unfair assumption but he was probably squeezed out when the old-timers returned to the business. :: Salz cites Oscar J. Friend, telling him that Thrilling needs "adult writing, mature characterization"; Ryerson Johnson, then with Popular Publications, credits pulp readers with wanting "adult stories as well as adult writing." This reflects the desire of pulp publishers to differentiate the product from the youth-oriented comic books eating into their business.]

MY AGENT SAID, "Now that you're here, I suppose you'd like to meet some of the guys who've been buying your stuff?"

"Why not?" said I (meaning I'd like nothing better).

He dialed numbers and talked to a few people, while I listened with bated breath. He talked to a guy named Leo, a guy named Don and several others. Rogers, the operator said, was home with the flu. He told the people he spoke to about a "visiting fireman" and arranged appointments.

In the next few days these appointments were consummated and the visiting fireman learned a few facts of editorial life that changed his entire viewpoint on writing. He learned that there was a new overall sweeping trend in the pulp detective field, a trend that was a hop-skip-and-jump ahead of most stories then being bought and published.

He learned that the editors were individually arriving at a new set of values in their quest for yarns.

I'll let the editors show you what I mean in a couple of minutes, but first let's start at the beginning. I had just rounded out my first year of professional writing when I made the New York visit. Stories written in that first year: 40. Stories sold: 27. A batting average of .675. That's fine in baseball, but writing stories ain't baseball. (Am I telling you!)

Object in going to New York: to find out just what additional punch was needed to bring my average of sales in the coming year up to 100%—well, maybe 80%. Also to meet my agent personally and find out what sort of guy he is. Also, to meet the editors and find out what they were.

"Elementary, my dear Watson!" you say. Right. Elementary. But boy, how we tend to forget the elementary stuff!

There were a few other questions on the mental list. For instance, what about the effect of the paper shortage on a writer like me? A writer just getting a grip on the bottom rung of the ladder? With a narrowing market, would the new writers be pushed out of the lineup by the veterans?

Also, there was the question of pulps vs. slicks. You know the one. It keeps popping up, and goes something like this: Will writing for the pulps over a period of years ruin your ability (if any) to write slicks?

Now for some answers, from the lips of the wise. That last question came up during lunch with August and Mrs. Lenniger. This was on my first day in New York, shortly after I had walked into his office and introduced myself. Until then, I had known my agent only through correspondence.

August, a blond-haired, forthright guy, with red-rimmed eyes that comes from reading stacks of mss., talks a dozen to my one, which suited me fine. Over Manhattans, consommé, ravioli, fruitcake and coffee, I shot questions at him with both barrels and he came across with the answers—until Mrs. L. had to take over, because August was neglecting his food.

Said August: "There's not a glimmer of truth in that old turkey that writing pulps will ruin your ability to write slicks. Just the opposite is true. Proof? Just a few names, men who started in the pulps and are tops in the slicks: C.P. Donnel, Jr., Allan Bosworth, Eddie Forester, Erle Gardner, Theodore Dreiser. You can take it from there. There's no better training for the slicks than writing pulps. A lot of what sells to the slicks is inferior to good pulps."

And to illustrate, he told me a couple of stories about yarns that were bounced by pulps and later, without revision, sold to slicks at rates that would knock you over. Let's not stick anybody else's neck out for them by naming names.

About the paper shortage, etc.? It's bad, and may get worse. Publications may use 75% of what they used in 1942. But a good story will always find a market—especially in the detective pulps. It boils down to the same old answer: If you're good, you'll sell.

"Human interest," says August. "Sympathetic people. Convincing human problems that pull the readers along from the word 'go' to finish. What Rogers Terrill calls 'emotional urgency.' "

There, brethren, are the opening notes of the editors' theme song. Let's ask 'em.

We're at the Standard offices—a plush layout, with a maze of big, airy offices. Modernistic decorations, thick rugs, deep chairs, enormous windows overlooking Manhattan's skyscrapers. The fellow I meet first is Oscar J. Friend, manuscript editor. He comes around an impressively enormous polished-top desk, offers his hand (a friendly grip and smile goes with it), and apologizes because Leo Margulies hadn't been feeling well and had gone home. Of course, that's disappointing, because I'd heard a lot about the legendary Leo, and had been anxious to meet him.

We light cigarettes and pitch in. Practically right off the bat, I get this information: Standard doesn't want slam-bang action stuff for the mere sake of action. What they want, Mr. Friend tells me, is adult writing, mature characterization, realistic backgrounds, *human interest*. There's that theme song.

"Of course," Friend declares in his Midwestern drawl, "if fast action fits into the story, if it's realistically motivated, then by all means use it. But action for its own sake is out. The important thing is suspense. You can have a scene in which no action whatever takes place—two men facing each other across a desk, as we are right now—and still you can build up terrific suspense."

A mild-looking, well-tailored little guy with a chubby face and quizzical eyes comes in, stands listening and nods his head. Mr. Friend introduces us and at last I meet Leo Margulies. He'd gone home, taken a nap and felt better, so he'd come back to the office. (You know that here is a man who really likes his work.)

The conversation becomes three-cornered and ranges over a variety of subjects. Remember, they're very busy guys, with stacks of manuscript to read, but they give you the impression that they have nothing more to do except sit around and educate the visiting writer.

Is there any particular type of story background they prefer, I wonder?

No. Use the background you know and understand. Set the stage in your own city, they tell me. And let the reader know it's your city. Mention familiar landmarks, department stores, street names. Readers have had enough of the New York City background, the overworked cop-and-gangster stuff.

Know the people you write about, and let them behave like human beings. You've heard that before and you'll hear it again. In the pulps it's a comparatively new trend.

What's the reason? The war is a big factor. Life is full of drama and excitement. A large percentage of pulp readers are the boys in the armed services. They know what it means to shoot and be shot at. Don't try to kid them with golden-hearted heroes who single-handedly (and often unarmed) mop up nests of two-legged rats. Many of today's readers know the meaning of real blood. Pulps are high on the reading list of G.I.'s.

Here's a thought that may occur to you. You've been reading some of the detective magazines and, b'gosh, you find plenty of whiz-bang stuff, little different from the yarns that were appearing a year ago. So you say, "Whoa, brother! Advice about breath of life and characterization sounds good in theory, but it just ain't the truth. Look at some of the yarns in the books!"

The answer to that is twofold. First, a lot of the stories on the newsstands today were bought months ago, maybe a year ago, before the new trend toward better, fuller fiction became well-defined. Stuff being used up from inventory. The second part of the answer: Editors just aren't getting enough of the kind of stories they'd like to buy, so naturally, they take the best of what they can get, even if the best is not exactly what they would prefer—especially when deadlines put on a little pressure.

What does Mr. Margulies have to say about the paper shortage? Well, it's bad, he admits. But the outlook for the future, after the war, looks extremely good.

"We've been through this before," he tells me, "and we know what a tremendous upsurge is coming in the publishing world. There will be flocks of new magazines to take the place of the ones that have disappeared from the newsstands."

But Margulies says he'll buy as many good shorts as he can get, even if there's no chance of using them for another year. With so many, many writers off to the army, as the married men tramp off, you can't blame an editor for trying to hoard up a few stories.

Well, I'd like to stay longer, but it's a good idea not to overstay your welcome. Besides, there's the appointment with Daisy Bacon, editor of *Detective Story*.

The new Street & Smith editorial layout occupies a floor of the Chanin Building, and the S&S reception office looks like you're coming into a svelte advertising agency. Modern furniture, thick rugs, high wide mirrors and a beautiful blonde. A guide took me to Daisy Bacon's office, which was just then being decorated, and I was introduced to her assistant, Ford, a young lady who looks mild and passive, but I suspect that after the manner of Dorothy Parker she reserves her comments until the visiting gentry have left.

We chatted about sundry matters and I realized that I had met Daisy Bacon before, in the pages of *Detective Story,* for her books, more than any others on the market, reflect the personality of the editor. Daisy Bacon likes the finer things in life, good books, good art, good theater. A gentle person who dislikes coarseness in stories as much as in life.

Too many writers, she believes, accent needless violence in their stories, and needless brutality to animals. "For example, there's the standby cliché in characterizing the villain, having him kick at a dog. It's not only oversimplified characterization, and hackneyed to boot, but presents unnecessary meanness to animals."

That recalled to mind a comment Rogers Terrill once made on one of my stories featuring a dog. "It's one thing to have human victims in a detective story—the reader expects that—but it brings in a decidedly unpleasant note when an animal is ruthlessly killed. It's almost as bad to some readers as killing off your hero!"

Incidentally, a type of story Daisy Bacon does not like is the one featuring a hunting background.

What sort of backgrounds *does* she like?

"Any that you know well and like to write about," she answers. "The background isn't the most important thing. The people are important. Make them real. Give them strong human problems."

Of the backgrounds that I'd used, were there any that she liked particularly? "Your small town newspaper background. That's a locale I can tell you're familiar with. And the Mississippi River background, as in that story of yours in my next issue—'She Walks In Terror.' I think it shows that you are thoroughly acquainted with that background and you were writing about something close to your heart."

You can't kid the editors with synthetic backgrounds. Well, maybe you can. I can't. The river has been my love and hobby ever since I was old enough to read Mark Twain's *Life on the Mississippi,* and walked down to the levee to find out for myself. There have been many trips on the river since then, on excursion boats, Coast Guard cutters, towboats. When you do that, and if it's something you really like doing, you can't help getting a pretty fair knowledge of the men who work on the river and what goes on in their hearts and minds.

Something Daisy Bacon said a couple of minutes ago: "Give your characters human problems." There's a variation on that familiar theme.

"Call it human interest," she says, "call it emotional impact, call it anything you wish. Labels aren't important. But what I want in stories is a sense of reality, convincingness and suspense."

That doesn't mean she wants the kind of yarn that starts with the hero on a street corner, a car careening around a corner, bang-bang! Somebody gets knocked off and the hero pitches in, willy-nilly, and for no good and logical reason, to find out who, what and why, the meanwhile being menaced all the way down the line by a lot of tough guys.

Menace? Sure, if it belongs. Action? Certainly, if it grows out of the story problem logically. But first of all, real people with strong human problems.

Is this getting monotonous? I'm only repeating what the editors told me.

Well, what is this mysterious thing called human interest?

Lenniger says: "A sympathetic character facing a problem we all recognize. Select a character with whom the reader can identify himself."

Somebody else said: "Human interest is derived from a character faced with one of the four 'universal' problems—loyalty, love, ego, or self-preservation."

What did Ryerson Johnson, of *Detective Tales,* say about this? "The strongest reader interest will be in a problem which hits close to home, a timely problem, or one which touches on the reader's own motivations."

This was during the course of a four-hour luncheon appointment at the Pen and Pencil Club. (It's a restaurant, but they call it a "Club.") "Johnny" Johnson is a thin man with dark, intense eyes. Mild, almost shy in appearance, straightforward, thoughtful and sincere.

"Your style is smooth," he commented, "but your plots are often still corny."

What's the remedy for the corn?

"Plotting is a matter of experience. The main thing, as I see it, is to let the action flow naturally out of your characters' problems. A lot of writers still have the idea that they have to write down to pulp readers. That's where they're making the biggest mistake. Pulp readers have grown up. They want adult stories as well as adult writing."

Somewhere during my hit-and-miss self-education in writing, I'd picked up the impression that a good complication story revolves around an unusual gag—a "germ" idea that sets your story apart from all others. That in your mind, you start with this "gag" and build your characters and plot action around it.

"That's like starting with the tail and adding a head and body as you go along," Johnson remarked. "There's nothing wrong with the gag idea—except that there's the danger of leaving the heart and soul out of your story when you try to mold your material over a skeleton built around a gag idea."

A couple of days later I heard the same thing when I went over to the Ace Magazines to talk with Donald Wollheim, editor of *Ten Detective Aces* and *10-Story Detective*.

"We have no objection to fast action," Wollheim said. "But it must be logical and not forced into your story because you may think that's what is wanted."

Well, that's a variation on the same theme. Boiled down, I'd say that what is wanted in the detective field now are strong human-interest stories with crime angles.

[*Writer's Digest*, September 1944]

A Yank at Yale
Staff Sgt. Mort Weisinger

[It seems every pulp author—or, in the case of Mort Weisinger, editor—dreamed of breaking into the slicks, where the money and prestige were so much better. Here, Weisinger (1915-78) describes his journey to the promised land while serving his wartime duty. Today Weisinger's reputation rests primarily on his editorship of the Superman comic books during the Silver Age.]

IT ALL STARTS ABOUT TEN YEARS AGO, back when you could buy a seven-course meal for fifty cents. Then, if you were a writer living in New York, you came around to the Friday luncheons of the old American Fiction Guild—providing you had fifty cents. If you'd had a bad week, you'd gripe about editors and talk about canning your agent. If you'd struck it well, you'd casually flash your checks before the envious eyes of fellow scribes.

I bet there isn't an agent breathing who wouldn't give ten percent of his remaining years to have under contract today the men who used to attend those luncheons. Under their own names, pseudonyms and "house" names, this group was responsible for at least nine out of every ten yarns in the pulps. George Bruce, Arthur J. Burks, Frank Richardson Pierce, Lester Dent, Paul Ernst, Ted Tinsley, Steve Fisher, Frank Gruber, Richard Sale, Jean Francis Webb and Frederick C. Painton. Today this roster sounds like a Who's Who of the big slicks and Hollywood's studios. But in 1934 they were all pulpsters, and for the privilege of rubbing elbows with these byline barons you had to have sold a minimum of 100,000 words to magazines of national circulation.

I was 19 at the time, writing my way through college grinding out pseudo-scientific stuff at ½¢ a word for *Amazing Stories,* Hugo Gernsback's old *Wonder Stories* and *Secret Agent X.* I wanted to become a surgeon, and fantasy tales were a byproduct of my science courses. As a hobby, I edited *The Time Traveler,* the first science fiction fan magazine. Harry Bates, editor of *Astounding Stories* when Clayton owned the title, used to help me get material for this little sheet, even though he wouldn't buy my stuff. One day he phoned his star contributor, Arthur Burks, arranged for me to interview him. And that is why I never became a doctor.

Mort Weisinger

I'll never forget the impression meeting Burks made on my unprofessional soul. He had just received his mail, slit open envelopes that contained twelve fat checks. Art let me soak up the glamour of his studio, talked shop, and invited me to call often. Months later, when I became eligible for membership in the AFG, he signed me up, brought me to one of their luncheons. Mixing with the writers, editors and agents there I wised up, organized a part-time agency of my own, handling science fiction only. It was while hustling for my clients in and out of editorial offices that I met Leo Margulies, chief at Standard Magazines. A short while later one of Leo's associate editors left, leaving him in a hole. He hired me to plug the dyke. I went after my degree at night, eventually decided that the only surgery I'd ever do would be cutting excess wordage on overwritten manuscripts.

I'm not going to take you through ten years of autobiography. I just want you to get the picture. The only world my friends and I knew was pulp. At Standard I helped edit thirty-eight pulp magazines. Every time I pressed a typewriter key, out rolled, "The body fell to the floor with a dull, sickening thud." *The Saturday Evening Post* was a Holy Grail, and a writer would not be above selling first serial rights to his wife's suicide note to rate a personal letter from a slick editor.

On this particular afternoon that it's taken me so long to revive for you, we were all buzzing over Fred Painton's bald announcement that he had just contracted to do a series of six short stories for *The American Magazine*. Of all the writers present at the table, two of them, both in their early twenties, seemed to be impressed the most. They were Steve Fisher, an ambitious ex-Navy lad turned writer, and Dick Sale, who had won a Street & Smith writing contest while a student at Washington & Lee, eloped with a childhood sweetheart, then came to New York to write murder stories. Made slick-conscious by Painton's success, Fisher and Sale made a bet with each other—as to which one of them would be the first to crack the *Post*.

After lunch, I went back to work, carrying a couple of novelettes that Burks had asked me to deliver to the office for him. (I often think the real reason Burks got me to join the Guild was so that I could deliver his scripts!)

I forgot the Fisher-Sale bet for about three years. Then one Wednesday I picked up a *Saturday Evening Post* and there, sure enough, was Fisher's byline on the table of contents. But the good-natured feud between Steve and Dick didn't end there. It had a twist. For, in the very same issue that carried Steve's short, the *Post* editors announced a four-part serial by Sale, to begin in the following issue!

I don't remember who paid who as a result of that bet, and it doesn't matter. Steve continued popping up in all the big slicks with a vengeance, as though making up for his 1¢ a word days in bondage, and soon hit the Hollywood jackpot. Sale didn't starve for slick credits, either. He wrote a very fine book, *Not Too Narrow, Not Too Deep,* sold it to Simon & Schuster. MGM bought it, switched the title to *Strange Cargo,* and featured Clark Gable in the lead.

And I guess everyone who reads the *Post* these days follows Sale's marathon-running "Alec" series there.

I mention Sale and Fisher because they were the slick trailblazers of our crowd. In the years to follow, Fred Painton shot up sky-high, became a fair-haired article writer for the *Post* and is now an accredited war correspondent for *Reader's Digest*. George Bruce, who used to be featured simultaneously on eleven different pulp covers a month, wrote a bang-up serial for Jack Byrne at *Argosy*—*Navy Blue and Gold*—sold it to MGM. They hired George to write the screenplay. The film made Jimmy Stewart—and its author. George is now in solid with Metro, earning a four-figure weekly salary.

Paul Ernst was next. He poured his pulp-earned pennies into a villa in Bucks County, and holed up there determined to hit the slicks. He made the grade admirably, selling first-class wares to the *Post, American, Country Gentleman* and others. Frank Pierce braked down on his western output for the pulps, became an institution with *This Week, Cosmopolitan* and *Liberty*. Ted Tinsley began topping his *Black Mask* detective yarns with romantic and adventure fiction in *American* and *Liberty*. Frank Gruber, holding down a job with a literary agent, devoted nights to book writing, turned out a flock of mystery bestsellers, won orchids from Walter Winchell, and now pecks a typewriter for RKO with the same results as though he were ringing up a cash register.

More years passed, and it seemed as if the world and his brother could hit the slicks—except yours truly. Summers I vacationed in Hollywood, where Bruce and Fisher would encourage me to take a stab at writing myself. Frankly, I was afraid to make the try. As an editor, I had read thousands of scripts running into astronomical millions of words. When you work over that much copy with a blue pencil, repairing motivations, patching plot flaws, highlighting clues, rewriting denouements so that they would sound convincing, something happens to your sense of perspective. Like a tool used too often, your judgment becomes blunted. You can't tell the corn from the green. Most of the plots I would work out in the leisure moments away from the shop I would reject in the typewriter as being too artificial. It's a fact that editors are tougher on themselves than on their contributors. Most of the clan will admit to buying stories they would never write themselves, but only because publishing exigencies demanded that the presses be fed.

Looking back, I guess it was all rationalization. Because there are dozens of editors who pound out top-notch salable copy in their spare time. Fulton Oursler found time to write his Thatcher Colt mysteries when he was editor of *Liberty*; Bill Fay edited a few pulps for Rogers Terrill over at Popular, knocked off sport stories for *Collier's* and the *Post* during weekends. Mary Day Winn, fiction editor of *This Week,* is the author of several books, manages to write pertinent articles on sociological problems for leading slicks. Edwin Balmer, chief of *Redbook*, collabs with Philip Wylie and others. Fanny Ellsworth, W.

Ryerson Johnson, Beatrice Jones and Oscar J. Friend are some of the other editors I know who can earn their salt at the writing racket if need be.

Once, when I asked the late A. Merritt, who was editor of the *American Weekly*, and authored such popular bestsellers as *Seven Footprints to Satan* and *Burn, Witch, Burn* how he managed to write after a day at the office, he answered: "I sit down to write only after I exhaust myself of all possible excuses."

Well, I kept thinking of damned good excuses as to why I shouldn't write, and this procrastination kept up for seven years, with time out only for an occasional house story when Leo wanted a yarn written around the cover, or when I needed a fast check for a payment on the car.

In 1941 Maj. George Fielding Eliot, who had been writing the G-Man book-lengths for us, gave up the assignment for greener pastures. George is one writer who really has a gift of gab, and being a military analyst on him looks good. I get a funny feeling whenever I hear him on the radio these days and remember how I used to give him plots for his Dan Fowler novels. Ed Churchill was one of the writers who took his place and when Ed went back to his publicity job at Paramount he recommended a friend, Whitney Ellsworth, for the chore. Ellsworth filled the breach admirably for three or four novels, then became editorial director of Superman, Inc., and his side output tapered down to novelettes and shorts. Like most writer-editors, he didn't write for the dough, but just to keep from going stale. At lunch one afternoon, Whit pointed out that of the fifteen comic mags his firm published, two of them alone, *Superman* and *Batman*, had a greater circulation than all the books put out by any pulp outfit, and mentioned that he needed an associate editor. I asked for the job, and got it.

It was a very good job and it paid so well that I shelved all thoughts of ever doing any extracurricular writing. It was a golden rut, and I would still be enjoying it if it weren't for the fact that two years later they picked a capsule with my number in it out of a fishbowl.

I told WRITER'S DIGEST readers in an article last year how the Army assigned me to Public Relations in Atlantic City with the Air Corps a few weeks after I was inducted. But the job wasn't steady and in February 1943 they transferred me to the AAF Training Command School here at Yale University. My duties consisted of writing publicity on the school for outside release and writing for the Post paper, *The Beaver*, published for several thousand aviation cadets.

You'd be surprised at the talent that has circulated through our Public Relations during the past year. There was Cpl. John Guenther, formerly aviation editor of *Newsweek*. Cpl. George Simon, ex-editor of *Metronome*, and brother of Dick Simon, of Simon & Schuster, is still here. Ditto for Pfc. Alan Waters, formerly New York correspondent for the *London Daily Mail*. And we've still got brilliant 24-year-old Cpl. Millard Lampell, who used to write the dramatic sketches for radio's *Green Valley, USA* series, the *Cavalcade of America* program, and *The Prudential Hour*. Hollywood stars we've had too in our campus foxhole. I roomed for several months with Sgt. Broderick Crawford and Sgt. Tony Martin. Maj. Glenn Miller, who used to direct our radio show here, just left for England. Lt. Bill Holden is our chief glamour attraction for the present. You're darned tootin' we're happy that the Army has given us an assignment corresponding with our civilian backgrounds. Who minds going overseas as long as they have you doing the job you know you can do best?

One day last year, while out on a "mission" with a class of photography cadets, I noticed that the cadets had parked their mobile photo trailer, of the type used in a theater of operations to develop aerial films, and had attached a rubber hose to the exhaust pipe of a jeep. The other end they inserted into a jug, filled with water from a nearby brook.

I asked Sgt. Lewis Greene, their instructor, what was cooking.

"Acid!" he replied. "The carbon monoxide fumes seeping through the water are changing it into a mild acid. Suppose the men are in a combat zone, and have to develop some aerial reconnaissance pictures in a hurry. They are out of acetic acid, needed to arrest development. By letting the exhaust from a jeep seep into a pail of water, the resultant liquid is a serviceable substitute. It's all part of the course here in Emergency Photography."

I took the course, and I became acquainted with lens-lore magic that would turn a professional photographer green with envy. Sgt. Greene had worked out a manual of ersatz chemicals that could substitute for many photographic necessities at the front, where material is often destroyed. He could teach the cadets how to take a picture without a camera—and develop it without a darkroom. He knew how to make a bar of G.I. soap take the place of sodium carbonate. He could make table salt, granulated sugar and an aspirin pinch hit for various chemical ingredients.

Here was wizardry indeed, wizardry that would warm the hearts of the taxpayers. Enthusiastic about this course in photo phenomena, I took the cover off the Underwood and began pounding away. I didn't stop until I had written 3000 words.

The resultant article, "Snapshots on a Shoestring," was sent to *Coronet*. When Harris Shevelson, the editor, wired back that he would use the article in their October issue, I knew I had something.

A carbon of the article was sent to *Life* magazine. *Life* was interested. They sent crackerjack photographer Andreas Feininger up here to Yale to do the story in pictures. For three days I worked with Feininger and Greene, helping prepare a layout that would tell the amazing story in full. *Life's* treatment of the story appeared in their issue of August 23, 1943, and ran three pages.

With *Coronet* and *Life* under my belt, I began slanting my stuff more and more at the national mags. I sat in on the School's chemical warfare course, cut enough meat out of it to write an article for Air Tech, "Death With the Wind." The Weight and Balance training given here, which teaches pilots how to load a plane properly, was crammed with Ripley facts. I tried to do this course justice in a long article, "They Didn't know It Was Loaded," and *Skyways* accepted it. Then followed a couple of articles for John Whiting of *Popular Photography*, a piece for *Air Force*, and a two-page spread for *PM's* Sunday Magazine section.

Civilian contacts came in mighty handy. Leo Margulies asked for and received a series for his air books on the various phases of our training program. I sold Lynn Perkins, a pal of mine on the editorial staff of *Parade,* on the idea of coming up to New Haven and lining up some picture stories on the school. For one of them, "On the Double or Nothing," which showed how accelerated is the training schedule for the cadets, he sent up photographer Peter Martin. Martin is the photographer who mugged "Commando" Kelly for his life story in the *Post,* and I had a lot of fun talking shop with Martin while he let me hold his extension lamp for him.

One stunt that I particularly enjoyed was getting Superman to come to Yale—literally. I dreamed up a rough outline for a story wherein Clark (Superman) Kent gets assigned to investigate training conditions at the AAF School at Yale for his paper. Whit Ellsworth came up here for the story conference, kicked the plot around until we had ironed out all the wrinkles. The finished product was a "Keep 'Em Flying" story that had Superman proving that the job of the ground crew technician can be just as glamorous as flying a P-38 through enemy ack-ack. And though he didn't give me any extra stripes for the job, they tell me that Maj. Gen. Walter R. Weaver, who was boss of our Command at the time, got a great kick out of the story when it appeared in print.

Yes, brother, that's how I got back in the magazine business, even though I was in the Army. Naturally, I couldn't receive payment for any of this copy, but I was glad to reap the bylines. *Coronet* did pay $150.00 for the piece I wrote for them, but the check, as well as all others, was turned over to the AAF Emergency Relief Fund. This is a regular army practice, very justifiable, and I quote from the Policy Book For Army Public Relations Officers:

> There is no objection to the practice of military personnel writing for publication and receiving remuneration therefor. Some rules, however, must be followed. A Public Relations Officer or a member of his staff may not receive pay for writing on a military subject since such writing is part of his duty.

Then one day it dawned on me. If I could crack national magazines writing for the Army, why not for myself? So one hot Sunday afternoon a year ago last July I rolled up my sleeves, immunized myself from the heat by swallowing some salt tablets, and tried a short-short. I mailed it, hopefully, to *This Week*. It was a light little yarn based on the radio character, Professor Quiz, only, for a twist, I had a Lady Quiz doing the quizzing. I was so surprised when *This Week* mailed me back a check for $450.00 for my 1400 words that I dropped my tray in the mess hall, spilling my entire chow over an innocent k.p.'s fatigues.

Having tasted blood, I replenished my supply of salt tablets, had the folks ship me my portable, and went on a busman's holiday five nights a week. I used my footlocker for a desk, and everything was fine, except that the guy in the upper of our double-decker would throw G.I. shoes at me when my typing kept him awake.

Studying the slicks, I noted that the majority of them were devoting more and more space to articles. The reading pendulum had swung from fiction to non-fiction. So I got in touch with Joseph Nathan Kane, a friend of mine who specializes in research and is the author of the reference books, *Famous First Facts*. I wrote Joe that I would like to do an article on famous inventions that were made possible by odd accidents and did he have any data? Joe told me where I could find the material in the Yale library. The result was an article, "Accidentally Ours," which *Coronet* purchased. They split it into four parts, ran it as a series.

Years ago I had stumped the experts on *Information, Please* with a trick question. Ever since, whenever I listened to the program and the oracles were stumped in an unusual way, I made a note of it in a little book. I also knew slick writer Gerrold Beim, whose wife, Lorraine, used to pick the questions for Dan Golenpaul when Canada Dry sponsored the program. A long talk with her, plus reference to my own notes, and I had material for a breezy article on how the sages are suckers for trick questions. Titling it "Misinformation, Please" I sent it off to *Coronet,* and back came another check.

Then, one day, the mountain came to Mohammed. Dick Lee, head of the Yale University News Bureau, tipped me off that Yale had just enrolled the youngest student ever to enter the school. He was 12-year-old Kenneth Wolf, who had an IQ of 197 and was so bright they had admitted him as a sophomore. But Dick had tipped off a lot of other guys, and when I arrived at his office to interview the prodigy, William Seabrook was there to cover the story for the *American Weekly, Toronto Star Weekly* had sent down one of their editors, and Universal Newsreels had him posing for the cameras. Then Don Halston, the local AP man in town here, managed to get me an exclusive interview with the kid's mother. It made for a scoop article. I called it "Brainchild" and *Magazine Digest* bought it.

At this point I took some time out for fiction again. Two yarns. They missed the slicks, but the pulps, God bless 'em, bought them with a few changes. I told Ray Palmer of Ziff-Davis that they were rejects, and he took one for *Mammoth Detective,* the other for *Amazing Stories*. And if you don't think that I didn't get a terrific bang out of seeing my name in the pulps again, after all these years, then take away my four stripes and bust me to private.

By November of 1943 I had milked my portable for more than $1200, which wasn't bad for four months of part-time writing. Thel, my wife, remained unimpressed, pointed out that the reason editors were buying my stuff was that all the good writers had been drafted and sent to Cooks and Bakers Schools.

In December I suddenly found myself devoid of ideas, afraid to stare a blank sheet of paper in the face. I decided I'd been working too hard, put in for a three-day pass. My wife, who is a registered nurse, took time off from her hospital, met me in New York. We were walking down 42nd Street when Jimmy Jemail, who is famous in these parts as the Inquiring Fotographer for the *New York Daily News*, stopped her, asked her "What do you do when your husband snores at night?" took down her answer, and photographed her for his column.

I got into a talk with this inquisitive reporter, discovered that no one had ever profiled him for a national magazine. I shunted the wife off to a movie and went back to the News office with Jemail. There I sweated out six hours with him, squeezed out material for a long article. I gave it everything I had, called the mss. "America's Nosiest Man," and sent it off to Ed Hutchings, Jr., of *Liberty,* who bought it for $300.00. A month after it was published, *Reader's Digest* picked it up for their July 1944 issue, condensed it down to two of their pages. The check from *Reader's Digest* was a whopper, netting me even more than *Liberty* had paid for the original article.

Times Square, where I had met Jemail, seemed to be a happy hunting ground for material, so I went back to the scene of the crime a month later. There's a famous little pawn shop on this street, Simpson's, and after a talk with the proprietor I wondered if the story of the Broadway celebrities who frequented this hock shop and anecdotes concerning them wouldn't make a good feature. I sent in an outline to *Coronet,* with a proposed title, "He Gives a Loan and Likes It," and they ordered it.

By this time Times Square had become my literary beachhead. There were a dozen stories camouflaged within the limits of this crossroads of the world begging to be unearthed, but they were all so obvious no one had ever thought of writing them up. There's a little newsstand there, for example, where you can obtain copies of newspapers from hundreds of different cities in America. Charles Hotaling, owner of this unique stand, told me how the FBI watches his site, frequently nabs "missing persons" who can't resist buying their hometown paper to see what's going on back home. Talking to Hotaling while he hawked his papers, I got a number of other interesting anecdotes. It was a natural, and I wrote it up in longhand on the train riding back to New Haven. I labeled it "400 Main Streets in Manhattan" and Dick Field, article editor of *This Week,* bought it on its first trip out.

And so it went. By July 1944, exactly one year after I had started at this part-time business, I had sold 17 different pieces to some of the country's top magazines, for a total of $3200. It'll be a pleasure to pay the income tax man his due on this take, for this writing spree proved a lot of valuable things. It convinced me, for one thing, that my years of apprenticeship in the pulps hadn't hurt a bit, and that Margulies' tutelage was paying dividends. And if you think it also didn't prove that the pulps are the logical stepping stones to the slicks, then I'll take my profits and buy Japanese war bonds with them.

They're talking now of the Army vacating Yale, which means that soon I'll be shipped out a long way from Times Square. But as long as I can get to my portable after duty hours, I don't mind. Now I've got the book bug, and I'd like to do a short psychological novel of a young kid coming back from combat. He's the sole survivor of a B-29, has seen his buddies die one by one and now, discharged from the Army, is trying to forget haunting memories and make the adjustment back to routine civilian life. It ought to be something writing that one. My Lord, it could be any of us.

[*Writer's 1949 Year Book*]

Hitch it to a Horse
Robert A.W. Lowndes

[Robert Augustine Ward Lowndes (1916-98), or "Doc" as he is affectionately remembered, had a prodigious career as writer and editor. He rose out of science fiction fandom, but was active in multiple genres. He was so productive, in fact, his output challenges the notion that there are only twenty-four hours in a day. He emerged in the early '30s as a letter-writing fan to the sf pulps. His first literary publication was a poem in William H. Crawford's semipro *Unusual Stories* (1935). In the late '30s, he was still a regular in the fanzines, participating in the great debates of the day. He appeared in titles like *Scienti-Snaps* and *Fantascience Digest* with both fiction and articles. In November 1940, Louis H. Silberkleit (~1905-86) and Harold Hammond restarted the old Double-Action Group (Winford, Chesterfield, Blue Ribbon, etc.) as Columbia Publications. Silberkleit had been president of Double-Action; made a fortune in comic books in 1939 and '40, while letting the pulp business slide. Under the new regime, Lowndes was hired to edit *Future Fiction* and *Science Fiction*. In 1942, he became managing editor of all the men's pulps (Marie Antoinette Park handled the love titles). He claimed that he became a editor because writing was "too hard work," but he continued to produce sf stories, publishing them in his own magazines and placing them with other publishers, as well. He wrote under dozens of pseudonyms, which continues to bedevil bibliographers. Eventually, he was as prolific in westerns as sf. At his peak at Columbia, he controlled about ten pulps. All were bimonthlies but, still, a lot of work. The pulps reeked of cheap on the outside: wrinkled spines, crooked wraps, drab covers. "This house is extremely open to new writers," he encouraged in 1952. Of course they were. Columbia had the lowest word-rates in the business (through no fault of Lowndes), making them a last resort for many seasoned professionals. Lowndes had read a bilge-load of stories by '52, when he'd had his fill of "space-pirates, giant insects, and swordsmen from Mars." He could have made similar disparagements in regards to the detective, western, and sports stories that landed on his desk. But despite his well-honed impatience, lovingly outlined below, Lowndes maintained a standard of quality in his magazines' fiction much better than Columbia's rates would have predicted. Thanks to Doc, in that regard Columbia was never cheap. He edited the chain well into the '50s, a long time after many had declared the pulps dead.]

Part One: *Inside, Looking Out*

1. The Mailman Cometh

According to an old and highly fallacious fable, a practicing editor is supposed to have acquired several layers of well-chilled lava around his heart.

After a few years on the job, nothing bothers him. He is reputed to be able to transfix manuscripts with a glance, and flip a rejection slip under the paper clip of an unoffending story faster than the fastest fictional two-gun man can draw his trusty cutters. He smells out a few name-writers and accepts their material while looking at a girlie calendar; he can't be bought in a crude way, but if you can pander to his pet foibles, you'll find that your stuff suddenly becomes acceptable. And so on and so on and so on.

We're all different individuals, with different tastes and temperaments—but there are some characteristics about us which are rather similar.

"Doc" Lowndes

One of these is that we don't like unnecessary work; and the daily deliveries of manuscripts to almost any editorial office is likely to bring forth a fair proportion of irritations, none of them necessary. All of these can be traced to one simple phenomenon: far too many persons who are trying to break into the writing field haven't bothered to learn the simple basic requirements for preparing and submitting manuscripts.

I haven't given up hope, vain as it may be, that I'll live to see the day when I do not receive stories addressed to magazines we no longer publish or to editors who haven't been with this company for years, or, worst of all, to editors or magazines connected with other companies. And, although the address of our editorial offices appears below the table of contents of each and every issue of our books, we still receive submissions forwarded from our printers. In some cases, there is an excuse—where a title has only recently been discontinued, an editor just recently left us; but in the great majority of instances, an examination of the story in question confirms the initial impression: lack of preparation for the job of writing.

When the mail is brought in, there are times when there won't be a clear spot on my desk, what with mss., layouts, proofs, etc., being spread out on it, but usually I take a quick glance before it is distributed to the staff. And, very frankly, I look for our "regulars" or for writers whose names are known to me. When one has a wide variety of choice, and limited time in which to choose, it's only natural to lean toward the already-tested. Such submissions are usually opened on the spot, and any personal notes to me read; once opened, they go into the "read right away" file. And with these will go short-short submissions from newcomers, where the envelope and manuscript itself show that the writer has taken some pains to present a readable piece of copy; he shows that he knows what he is doing.

The rest are put aside for later opening and consideration. These include submissions to magazines presently overstocked (and, to be fair, a writer cannot be blamed for not knowing about such a condition in many cases); novelette-size envelopes addressed to books which do not use novelettes, etc. And at the bottom of the pile go the offerings whose physical appearance is against them.

2. Open the Envelopes, Richard

After eight years, I still can be amazed at some of the envelopes we get. You can blame those couriers who remain undaunted by rain, snow, fog, gloom of night, etc., for some things, but it isn't the mailman's fault if a writer has jammed a thick script into so small an envelope that the package seems to be on the verge of bursting. Obviously, the return envelope with such submissions isn't going to be any larger. So you root around your desk for a large envelope and address it for the author.

This unnecessary work, curiously, makes for far more irritation than you would think; it's the grain of sand in the shoe, which, according to legend, wears down the traveler more surely than the length of the journey.

First impressions are not necessarily sound ones; often they're unfair. But we live in a civilization where we've been trained to react quickly; our nervous systems are pretty well set in various established patterns, and no matter how hard we may try, consciously, to delay our reactions and not to jump to conclusions, a certain amount of signal-response is going to happen anyway. My unconscious response to manuscripts which do not contain the full names and addresses of the writers, or which are sloppily typed, or which show that they've been knocking around for quite a while is bound to be unfavorable. This initial judgment is justified so frequently that I'm likely to stop with it, if I lack time for further investigation. These clues suggest lack of basic interest in learning how to go about becoming a writer. Exceptions exist, but they're few and life is too short.

There is one kind of manuscript which gets put back into the envelope and returned at once, and that is the submission which is typed single-space or is handwritten. Even if the stories thus submitted were good (and this is generally unlikely) such manuscripts would have to be typed or retyped for the printers. We do not have the facilities for doing this kind of thing, and it isn't the editor's job.

"But is this fair to writers?" someone is bound to ask. "Shouldn't *every* story be considered, anyway?"

My answer is a plain, flat "no." It's not a question of "fairness" to begin with; we're not playing games; we're trying to run a business. No amount of sympathy for writers, and I have quite a bit of that, can evade the basic fact that persons writing for magazine publication are trying to sell commodities. It isn't a matter of "art"; we pay money for stories which we believe will sell the magazines by appealing to our readership—but we see no point in examining shoddy-looking material in hopes of salvaging something from it. If you went into a store where the merchandise was sloppily arranged, dusty, the price tags either missing or mixed up, etc., would you patronize the store on the proposition that it wasn't fair to the shopkeeper not to give his goods a trial? (Actually, in some cases, you might overlook a genuine bargain, but an editor's life is paced by deadlines and lack of time prevents browsing for bargains.)

The astonishing thing is that although the writers' magazines have made this point innumerable times before, events at editorial offices show that it has to be repeated.

3. No, That's Not a Likely Story

Almost anyone is likely to wonder, now and then, if the stories sent to editorial offices are actually considered. I can't speak for any other offices (although from what I've heard, editorial practices in the pulp field are more or less consistent), but let's go into what is meant by "considering" a story before I try to answer the question. "Consideration" simply means determining whether the manuscript in question can be used by any particular magazine.

Obviously, consideration in some cases will be so brief as to be non-existent; for example, there's no point in reading an adventure story at our offices, no matter who wrote it, because we do not have any adventure story magazines; the same goes for air-war stories, fantasy, weird, or science fiction stories, romantic western stories, historical-background stories, other than those dealing with the period of the American West between 1848 and 1900, and so on.

And there's no percentage in reading manuscripts which are the wrong lengths; we use short stories up to 5000 words; western novels and love novels between 40,000 and 45,000 words; and a few sports and western novelettes between 8000 and 12,000 words. Once in awhile, we'll take a short story between 5000 and 6000 words, or a 7000 or 14,000 or 15,000-word novelette—but this is rare. There's an occasional use for a love novelette; we don't use detective story novelettes. We may, at times, consider a 6000-word short story from a regular writer, with the possibility of its being cut down in mind; but, on the whole, it's a waste of time and energy to read the off-lengths.

All these facts about our requirements are apparent to those writers who study our magazines as markets.

I'd like to be able to send out letters to the regular contributors about changes, when they happen, but it often just isn't feasible; after all, picking the manuscripts and working with writers is only a third of an editor's job; the magazine has to be produced and production takes up most of the time available. When I can, I'll jot a note on rejection slips advising of changes, but, here again, it can't be done all the time.*

4. *"You Don't Have to Eat a Whole Egg to Know That It's Bad."*

George Bernard Shaw is supposed to have used that line on a tyro who sent him a bulky manuscript, certain pages of which had been fastened together so that the writer would know approximately how far he'd gone in reading it.

Even if it were possible for every manuscript suitable for consideration to be read all the way through, this would be a superfluous labor, and an unintelligent procedure to boot. The sad truth of the situation is that there are many persons trying to become selling writers who have not yet attained the necessary proficiency. And, sadder still, no one has told them—or they've refused to believe it when told; many with the "talent" haven't developed it. There is hope, but editors can't do much about them. Other channels, many of them reliable and worthwhile, exist for the potentially capable.

At any rate, the thoroughly "hopeless" manuscript can usually be spotted by page three, and frequently a glance over page one is enough. But, might not a story improve after a weak beginning, some still ask? Yes—it might. But I'm not running a writer's school; I'm trying to pick out the best available to me in *finished products*. You may disagree with me on the results in some cases, but that's beside the point. Likely as not, when you're reading, you use a similar approach; if you're picking out a book to give to someone, you probably won't take one which, to your taste, starts out poorly, with the proviso that "it might pick up interest later on." And I'm not *giving* the books away.

Oh, but shouldn't I give the newcomer a break—shouldn't I read the story all the way through? How will I find new blood if I expect the best from people who haven't sold before?

Every year, not only in my books, but in the pulps of other companies, writers who have never sold a story in their lives "break in." Why? Because the manuscript *is* up to the requirements; it may not be as good as the best in

---

* What does "production" mean? After an editor selects a story, here's what else he does with it: (1) Dictates a note accepting it. (2) Okays purchase voucher for the cashier. (3) Inspects the check before it's mailed to verify the rights that are being purchased. (4) Edits the script and does what revision is necessary. (5) Has certain facts in the ms. double-checked. (6) Either okays the title or creates a new one. (7) Talks with the artist about an illustration and layout. (8) Sends the ms. to the printer. (9) Schedules the story in the proper issue. (10) Thinks up a promotion angle for the story if he can. (11) Writes a subhead. (12) Checks galley proofs, then page proofs, then folios the pages and writes captions for the illustrations. (13) Answers fan mail on the story. (14) Encourages the author to "come again" if the story was a good one.—WYB editor

these magazines, but it meets the minimum, at least. Obviously, even the top regulars do not turn out their best work each and every time; you know that from your own reading. There's no ceiling on how "good" a pulp story can be within the general definition of pulp fiction, but there's a floor on the question of how "good" it has to be to be usable. Some newcomers start in with higher standards of productive quality than others; some just make it the first time, and pick up later on.

5. Sorry—not for us!

"Well," someone is bound to ask by now, "a 'good' story will be accepted, won't it?"

We have to qualify that phrase before we can continue any farther; we have to make it "good pulp story." Because I receive a fair number of "good stories" which are not "good pulp stories." (See part two for elaboration on "good pulp story.")

Then, there are a fair number of "good pulp stories" which just are "not for us." Examples would be western stories with Indian War plots, with Indians, Mexicans, Chinese, etc., as the main villains, etc.—stories of a kind some other houses use, but which violate our own particular taboos.

Can manuscripts which have come back because of overstock situations be resubmitted later? The answer to that is generally "yes," but it's a good idea to query first, unless I've already invited resubmissions in WRITER'S DIGEST or one of the other writers' magazines.

The mention of "good stories" brings up a routine writers' beef. "You rejected *my* story," they say, "yet in your latest issue of such-and-such you published something I'd be ashamed to put my name to. Why do you say you want good (don't forget those quotation marks)—'good' stories, when you returned mine and published this (words missing)?"

Let's assume that the complaint is justified in that this story which we returned was better than the one we published; let's go farther—let's say for the sake of argument that the story returned was very "good."

This sort of thing happens—and to the best of my knowledge and belief it's likely to happen anywhere: a story which is "good" by the standards of the editor in question will be returned and a poorer story by the same standards accepted. Why? Because no editor I know of is at his best in judgment *all* the time; he's likely to accept a story today, then beat his head against the wall later. But I don't think many, if any, of my colleagues enjoy (or suffer from) delusions of grandeur.

Readers quickly beat it out of us. You'll find imperfect editorial judgment somewhere on almost every printed magazine page.

No matter how carefully an issue is planned, there's a possibility that, at the very last moment, we'll find ourselves confronted with a void aching to be filled. Frequently, there's somewhat less than no time at all in which to fill it, and at that time, it sometimes happens that, instead of holding out for the best, we just have to compromise with the "least poor." These "desperate remedies" will not be as good as a story we returned, perhaps regretfully, some time back.

On the other hand, this kind of situation sometimes offers a break for a newcomer, and I've "discovered" a few pretty good ones at moments of crisis. Fortunately, these situations do not happen every month, and one reason why they don't is because I keep an eye out for "good" short-short stories. Here's where the unknown writer has his best opportunity, because the "regulars" rarely write that length (except for professionals who specialize on short-short stories and articles). And it's only natural that once a "find" is made, I'll look forward to more material from the fledgling, in hopes that this one good job wasn't just a happy accident.

Now and then, people ask me: "Aren't most writers just a little 'off'?" Well, there are many persons making a living from pulp writing, or contributing material on a part-time basis, but you won't find any "writer" type any more than you'll find a "lawyer" type. They're all individuals and most of them likeable people, personally. If some of them may appear to be a little "off," at times—well, it's a strange business.

And I've been asked, too: "Aren't most editors difficult to deal with?" I don't know "most editors" personally, but I do know that there isn't any "editor" type, either. *I'm* difficult to get along with, at times—and if you know any human being who isn't, *don't* tell me about him; if such a person exists, I'd rather remain in relatively blissful ignorance about him or her.

In what other profession can a man, having served little or no apprenticeship, and with no academic degree, and perhaps devoid of all "salesmanship" in his personality, suddenly hit with a novel that brings worldwide fame and wealth to his home? And in what other profession do people keep trying year after bitter year to break in? In most trades or professions, a few "no's," and the aspirant changes his ambitions. But in writing they hang on and on, and then, suddenly, they click with every editor. What kind of people would you expect such a profession to attract? Certainly imagination and persistence are their trademarks.

Part Two: *No Royal Road*

1. Writing is a Business

Just as every citizen is supposed to know the law, and ignorance thereof isn't acceptable as an excuse (regardless of how unfair this may be at times), the simple fact that you submit stories for professional consideration implies that you know what you're up against. If you don't, it's too bad, but well-meaning ignorance will not help; and one of the basic matters which it is assumed you must know is the state of the market; what kind of stories are being bought *now*; what lengths, etc.

You can't find out market conditions, *once and for all*, in regard to the pulp field in general, or any publisher or individual editor or specific magazine in particular. What *was* true six months ago is not necessarily the case today.

So far as general policy goes, reading "current" issues is fairly reliable. You have to learn how to "read," which involves getting the maximum of information with a minimum of time-expenditure. Obviously, you cannot read each and every issue of every pulp magazine, or even every sports, western, etc., book, and still have time for writing, Therefore, you pick representative samples each month: if your field is sports, then buy one issue of each editor's sports magazine for which you are writing, and analyze at least one feature-story and one short story of the kind of sports you most generally write.

You cannot tell from the date on the issue *when* that story was bought, or whether it represents a "typical" example of what the editor wants; however, you can develop a fairly good instinct for sound diagnosis with practice and alertness. And, if you are in touch with the editor, you could ask him if such and such a story is an example of what he really likes best in such and such respects; characteristics of a given story might indicate a change in the market, or they might be atypical—the story might have been accepted in spite of rather than because of these matters.

When I was trying to break into the writing game some years ago, one thing that bewildered me was to read in various writers' magazines, and to hear from personal conversation, that such and such an editor wanted this, that, and the other—then to find a number of stories in the current issue, which, as far as I could see, just didn't contain this, that, and the other, at all.

One veteran of the alleged "blue pencil" (strangely, I've yet to come across an editor who actually uses the legendary "blue pencil"), told me, yes—you're right. These stories *do* contradict what I've told you; I think they're good stories, but they were not what I really wanted. But I can't hold off and wait for a full issue of exactly what I want; I tell writers these things, hoping to get them, but when deadline comes, I have to put a book together and I often have to compromise and take the best available. At the time, I thought this was a bit feeble and was sure that if *I* ever became an editor—now I'm certainly a little sadder, at least.

Exactly how you get the "savvy," the ability to make sound predictions from studying current issues, is something which no one can tell you. All I can tell you here is *don't stop studying*; don't, once you make a sale or two, decide that you "know what's what" now and assume that you'll keep selling from here on out. Paderewski is supposed to have said that if he missed one day's practice, he could tell the difference; if he missed two days, his wife could tell; if he missed three days, the critics spotted it; and if he took a week off, everyone knew it.

2. Some Characteristics of a "good pulp story"

Note that word "some"; if this section were as long as the complete article, it would still not cover *all* the characteristics of our abstract "good pulp story." I consider the ones I list as essential, but this does not mean that you will sell any and every story faithfully containing all of these, or that you might not read in print (or, at times, even sell yourself) a story where one or more of these were absent. But you *can* depend more often upon seeing these characteristics in a "salable" story than on not seeing them.

The "good pulp story" revolves around *one* central character, presented in such a way that the "reader" will be interested in finding out what happens to him; generally, he should be "sympathetic" in that his likeable qualities will overbalance other aspects of him; but, a character, who will be disliked enough that the reader wants to see him get it in the neck, fulfills the requirement, too.

The "plot" of the story revolves around this character, rather than the character being tailored to fit a plot. The story opens with this character *involved* in a situation where he is seemingly up against something he cannot handle— although, for some understandable and interesting reason, he *must* handle and overcome it. Being "human," he has weaknesses as well as strengths, and, in these circumstances, his strengths appear to be of little help to him; he tries to tackle the situation and succeeds only in getting in deeper.

A series of related incidents, arising believably from the combination of the initial situation and the hero's character, lead to further attempts to solve the problem; they are seemingly successful up to a point, then—failure. When a crucial moment occurs, where if he fails there won't be another chance, he succeeds; he does so through his own efforts, through overcoming his weaknesses and turning them into strengths, etc. He may have assistance, either at the end, or from the very beginning, but at the "climax," the *lead*, and not someone else, turns the trick.

Now, let's become more specific on each of these points.

(a) The story must begin on page one—not page three or four—and this means that by the end of that page the "hero" must have been introduced, *some* of his essential character revealed, and the general nature of the problem (if not the problem itself) shown. Examples:

> (1) He went into his backhand corner and dug out that low-bouncing

chop shot. A drive straight down the sideline could be a placement. Dangerous, of course, with the pellet likely to go out at any point. Then Long Joe Palme remembered the Tessard court strategy; never give an opponent a chance at the big angle unless you know you've got him passed. So Long Joe held himself in, throttled his normal what-the-hell, shoot-the-works attitude and stroked it deep to the center of Judge's baseline. Judge was one of the fastest men in the game, capable of retrieving a ball to any part of his court. But Long Joe swore under his breath as he gave up the gambling opportunity. ("Bulldog on the Baseline" by T.W. Ford, *All Sports*.)

(2) Luke Crowder didn't want to kill old Hodge Aikens. Not that Luke had any love in his heart for the old man. It was just that old Hodge, even with sixty winters behind him, was still doing most of the work on the quarter-section homestead, and Luke knew that with Hodge gone life would be a little harder. But Luke figured he had to kill him or stretch a hangrope himself, and to Luke's way of thinking, that didn't leave him much choice.

That was why Luke was chopping the stove wood this morning. Hodge usually took care of that chore, but Luke slipped out early and split up enough wood to cook a meal. A crafty smile spread over Luke's weasel face as he picked up the armload of jack oak. Hodge didn't know it but he was about to build his last fire in the old cast-iron stove. ("The Gravemaker" by Dan Kirby, *Famous Western*.)

Example one gives you a sympathetic lead, Long Joe Palme in a situation where his natural style of playing is in conflict with what is expected of him; the general problem is outlined, the specific difficulty (this present game) setup. We don't know yet *why* Long Joe *must* be involved in this way, but there is sufficient interest *and story-motion* in this first paragraph to carry the reader along.

Example two introduces a believable character, Luke Crowder, who is not sympathetic; he has to solve the problem or hang, and his solution will be murder. We know at the end of the second paragraph the general method he will use, although not the full details. But, again, there is sufficient interest and story-motion to carry the reader on—we want to see Luke fail and get what's coming to him.

In both cases, we have universal situations—nothing outré or over-melodramatic; anyone *might* be up against either or both types of situations.

(b) Reporting is not fiction writing; a story, as you may have heard before, is a meaningful sequence of emotions, not just a sequence of facts. Without the emotion, without the personal feelings of the lead, and of other people in the story, the motivation for their actions, their attitude toward them, you merely have an article in narrative form, at best. You have good journalism, perhaps, but not fiction.

Let's take the reportorial context of the paragraph quoted from "Bulldog on the Baseline."

> He went into his backhand corner and dug out that low-bounding chop shot. Long Joe stroked it deep to the center of Judge's baseline. Judge was one of the fastest men in the game, capable of retrieving a ball to any part of the court.

Many beginners would have thought that this was all that was needed; and the paragraph still has color, but it has now become impersonal. We have two "characters," Long Joe and Judge; we have action. But we do not have any feeling or motivation; it's merely a well-presented description of part of a tennis game, which may be of interest to people who like to read descriptions of tennis games, but it has no story-meaning; Long Joe is a puppet batting the ball back and forth across the net. Change his name to Big Bill, and he has as much meaning.

But when the omitted sentences are added, Long Joe becomes a distinct individual; we not only know that he's playing against someone named Judge, (who, at this instance hasn't any profile), but we know a little of *how* he is playing, *why* he is playing this way, and how Long Joe *feels* about it. We know he'd much rather be playing some other way. Those added items are the sort of thing that make the difference between fact and fiction.

(c) Involvement in a situation does not merely mean taking the character and letting things happen to him; there must be meaning in what happens and a credible relationship with your lead's motives and goals. The reason for your hero's involvement must spring from his character and from his motives—from choices he has made before the story opened; the legendary bolt-from-the-blue will not suffice, unless the probability of lightning was inherent in the lead's motives and behavior in the past.

In the story above, Long Joe is in conflict because he chose to adopt a discipline of tennis strategy which was unnatural to his style of playing; that we can see. Later in the story, we find out that Long Joe was trying to fit himself into this wrong-shaped hole because he wanted to make time with a girl in the tennis social set; and in order to do that, he had to change himself.

In the second story from which we quoted, we find a little later on that Luke had killed a storekeeper in town, while trying to rob the man; the storekeeper had recognized Luke and shouted out his name.

> Luke was just slipping out the back door into darkness when he saw old Hodge coming down the alley. He knew it was Hodge by the stiff-jointed gait of the man. He and Hodge had ridden into Iron Post together

that evening to take on supplies. There was no moon and Hodge's eyes weren't sharp as a squirrel hunter's any more, but Hodge could hear. Hodge could hear like a black-tailed deer. Luke knew that Hodge must have heard Chet Long call out his name. Hodge would have thought nothing about it right then, but later, when he heard that Chet Long was murdered about the time he and Luke were in town. . . .

Now we have specific and immediate reason for Luke's murderous plans toward old Hodge; it doesn't make Luke any more likeable, but it does make him, his actions and motives more understandable. We know that he isn't just a victim of circumstances; the first paragraph alone might have left a bit of sympathy for Luke, but now we know that we want him to fail in his attempt and take the consequences of his previous actions as well. (Until then, it might have been possible for Luke to have a change of heart at the last moment, and for his past trouble to have been a case of justifiable homicide, etc., or false accusation, etc.)

These factors give a feeling of inevitability, basic for strength and purpose in fiction. Without them, the happenings are arbitrary; various other events could just as easily take place without it making much difference. In the "real" world, much of what happens seems purposeless and arbitrary, but in fiction—at least in pulp fiction—there must be a believable structure to the story, a discernible reason for everything that happens.

(d) The final solution must rise out of elements already given, even if they have been toned down. Theoretically, it would be sound for the hero to solve things at the end by wiggling his ears, providing that his ability to wiggle his ears had been mentioned before. But one very frequent flaw in otherwise "good" stories is the *deus ex machina* ending; not very many beginners resort to the sudden appearance of the rich uncle, the marines, or the earthquake to come in at the right time. (Incidentally it's okay to have the marines come in at the end *if* the lead has already taken over on his own before they arrive.) But the sudden introduction of any important element not mentioned before (hero suddenly wiggles ears), the entrance of characters not introduced before (marines, rangers, etc.) or the hero's finally being saved by any means outside his own efforts, constitutes a "god out of the machine" and makes the story curl up like last week's lettuce. That doesn't mean, of course, that the protagonist has to do everything himself, but merely that someone else cannot solve his problems *for* him.

(e) Every character is a distinct individual, not a "type," and the story must deal with people, not with labels. In western stories, "cattleman," "sheriff," "outlaw," "banker," "gambler," etc., represent useful classifications of the various social groupings within which many, if not most, of the characters in the stories will fall. But the classification, the label, is *not* the person; to say that John Doe is a "gambler," for example, is to relate only a little information about what John Doe does for a living; the label "gambler" *omits most, if not all, of John Doe's individual characteristics.* Similarly with racial, religious, or political labels, etc. Nor is such a label sufficient grounds for predicting a character's behavior in any-and-all situations.

It is stereotype "characters," rather than similarity of plots and backgrounds, which can give a cut-and-dried monotonous sameness to any type of story. Thus, were you to analyze a large number of stories from the desk of any given, first-rate, western story writer, you might be astonished to find how similar the stories are in plot, and yet how fresh each individual story seems. The next time you read a western story which gives you the feeling that you've read this stuff dozens of times before, look and see if it isn't a case of "stock" characters, puppets walking around with signs on them, rather than believable people reacting to familiar situations in an unfamiliar way.

3. You Don't Start Just Anywhere

Writing pulp fiction is not, among other things, a "mission." It isn't a vehicle for sermonizing; it hasn't a "purpose" so far as divulging great "truths," etc., is concerned.

This does not mean that you cannot, or won't, put some of your own beliefs and/or attitudes into your stories; if you are creating characters, rather than filling in blanks, you can't help putting a fair amount of your own feelings into your work.

If you try to make your fiction fit the requirements of *any kind* of "line," then the chances are you won't have good fiction, although you may have effective propaganda. It's the difference between letting your personality come out and express itself in your stories (which is healthy), and forcing your fiction into a predetermined mold from the beginning.

The place to start is where you feel most "at home." Write the kind of stories you enjoy reading yourself—but don't aim at the very top to begin with. The old saw about hitching your wagon to a star sounds very well but if you want to get somewhere, you'd better hitch it to a horse, or some other contraption that stays on the ground and knows where it's going.

In each of the several general classifications of pulp fiction, you will find a fairly large variety of kinds-of-story. Pick the one you find most sympathetic to *you* for a start; you can enlarge and raise your standards after you get going. But if you try to beat the top writers on their own grounds to begin with, the chances are you'll be beaten by other newcomers who were willing to serve an apprenticeship.

Thus, in beginning, keep away from the "timely" story—the story built around news events and "issues" of the day; you see this kind of story in print, but it is nearly always done on assignment by top names; for every one you see, there are many unsolicited examples rejected. Keep away from the "off-trail" story, at first. These are usually done by arrangement, and require special information not available to you under present circumstances. (What is "off-trail" for one market, of course, may not be so for another; for example, I use some humorous western and sports stories, while certain other editors will not. But even here, I can only use a very few, and each one you read in my magazines probably represents a dozen or more which were sent back.) After all, if you break in there's a fair chance that you can stay in, and if you do, you'll get your chance at the "off-trail" material. ("Off-trail" is generally differentiated from "taboo" in that occasionally the former kind will be used, while the latter is unusable. A western story from the heroine's viewpoint would be "off-trail" for me, while a western story revolving around warfare between the U.S. Army and the "savage redskins" is taboo.)

4. If You Don't Like It Here—Leave!

Pulp magazines are published for a mass audience, at middle levels of general intelligence and literary taste; they do not pretend to be anything more than vehicles for entertainment and relaxation, and the "literary" level isn't of prime import. You will find *some* very good writing in the various magazines, some rather poor writing; but most generally, the writing will be of medium excellence—which is what the term "mediocre" actually means. Thus you need not try to acquire a "style" similar to that of the masters of English literature—but on the other hand you do not have to be afraid to write as well as you can. What is generally required is a style and *pace* that moves along quickly: you cannot stop the action of the story for introspection or philosophy as may be found in Tolstoy or Proust. (But if you've never read Tolstoy or Proust, and all in literature that those two names imply, your writing is the worse for it.) You cannot get away with writing down.

Many persons, feeling the "urge" to write, have a very low opinion of pulp magazines and of pulp writing; they consider it beneath them and condescend only to start out in this field. Whether you should feel "above" writing for the pulps is none of my business; it's your affair. But it *is* my business, and the business of any other pulp editor, if you are wasting our time by expecting us to read stories you've written with your tongue stapled to your cheek. And such an attitude will show up and show you up much quicker than you imagine. (Some have gotten away with it, but the odds are against *your* doing it.)

It isn't necessary for any pulp writer to feel that this is the finest branch of literature, and I don't believe that very many, if any, of the regulars do. Part of understanding any form of writing involves understanding its limitations and restrictions, and the sensible course is to do work you're not ashamed to sign your name to within these limitations. I doubt if any of the big-time writers who started out in the pulps are now haunted in their sleep by their early stories—*not if these stories were honest expressions of the best they could do at the time.*

The field of commercial writing is a large one, and, if you want to get into it and stay there, you owe it to yourself to find out what it embraces. If you have what it takes to meet the requirements of any particular branch of the writing field, then you'll arrive sooner or later; the sane course is to pick a branch where there's room for newcomers—some fields are broader than others—and start there. After all, writing is one of the few vocations where it is possible to "earn while you learn"; you can start learning at any time; it requires patience, a capacity for self-criticism, and plenty of guts.

[*Writer's Digest*, November 1950]

The Good Life

[What seems like a trifle now, seemed magical in 1950, a pulp magazine being edited from Los Angeles, a faraway place not to be found on maps of New York or Chicago. This momentous event in the prehistory of telecommuting had been mentioned several times in *Writer's Digest* before receiving the below write-up, with accompanying cover credit and photo spread. :: Irma Ginsberg graduated Phi Beta Kappa from Syracuse University, class of '45. She appears to have started at Popular Publications as secretary to president Harry Steeger. In another capacity, she assisted Peggy Graves, editor of *New Love* and *Romance*, while also publishing stories under the name Diane Austin. Current information gives her some two-dozen credits between January '47 and June '54, the majority of them in Popular's *Rangeland Romances*. In June '47, a new western love title was announced, with Harry Widmer as editor. By early '48, editing responsibilities had been handed over to Irma. Requirements called for stories from the heroine's point of view, with authentic western flavor. Furthermore: ". . . heroines can be somewhat more forward than those of the usual love story. Let them go after their men and capture them by any means fair to romance—which means any at all. Writing may be a bit spicy and intriguing, but never in poor taste . . ." The new magazine, *Romance Western*, debuted with an April '48 cover date and a bimonthly schedule. Soon after, Irma married Austin "Rocky" Kalish, a writer for *The Martin and Lewis Show* on NBC radio. When the show moved to LA, the Kalishes followed, Irma taking *Romance Western* with her. While the upbeat "The Good Life" was being published, the pulp was actually in its last throes. It changed title to *Romance Western Roundup*, delayed an extra month, and added a reprinted story every issue. All three were bad signs, hinting at the magazine's struggle in the crowded western love market. In its new guise, it lasted only three issues. But the move to LA paid off for the Kalishes. The husband-and-wife team wrote for an early television show, *Meet Corliss Archer*. In late '52, Rocky became one of the head writers for *The Martin and Lewis Show*, replacing Norman Lear. The couple collaborated on scripts, both on radio, and on TV when Martin and Lewis hosted *The Colgate Comedy Hour*. Thus began a remarkably successful television career for the couple. They've scripted over 300 episodes for *Gunsmoke*, *My Three Sons*, *My Favorite Martian*, *F Troop*, *All in the Family*, and many other shows. And never in poor taste. In the '70s, Irma became a female pioneer in the industry by producing a number of series, starting with *Good Times* (1974). In essence, she made the transition from the pulps to a medium that supplanted them. The couple are currently prestigious members of the Writers Guild of America, well-known for their charitable endeavors. Irma's most recent writing project is a mystery novel, *As Dead As It Gets* (Forge Books, 2006, written under the name Cady Kalian with co-author Naomi Gurian), with a followup due in August '07. And that's a happy ending to match any of Irma's love stories.]

NOTHING—NOT EVEN THE EDITORS' HONEYMOON—can keep a magazine from going to press. Two years ago, Irma and Rocky Kalish were married in New York, then rushed out to California to meet a deadline on *Romance Western*—their unusual wedding present.

What does a publisher do when one of his most capable editors gets married and moves 3000 miles away from home base? Harry Steeger, of Popular Publications, had the answer. He let Irma take her magazine with her—that's how *Romance Western* came to be the only Western pulp edited in the West.

Irma had been editing the book for only a short time and the move was unprecedented, but, as Harry Steeger says, "Irma and Rocky are a couple of smart kids. When you stop to think of it, it could be a gargantuan headache to have a book scheduled from New York, printed and distributed from Indiana, and edited from California.

"That it isn't, is as complete a tribute as I can pay to the editor. When we started, the idea of isolating one of our 38 magazines and operating it by remote control seemed to be asking for trouble. Actually, there's been no trouble at all. Manuscripts submitted to *RWR* are read, screened and accepted in Los Angeles, vouchered, illustrated and paid for in New York. The Kalish team reads galleys and foundry proofs, corrects them, and mails them straight to the printer."

Steeger talks affectionately of Irma: "She was one of the most brilliant editorial people we ever had in our N.Y. office. Irma used to write one or two stories a week, and accomplish all her editorial work besides. But her genius for doing things expertly doesn't end there. When she and Rocky were in New York last spring, they brought with them the happiest baby girl we've ever seen. She sat in our office for an hour or two and never cried once. She'll make a good author some day."

Baby Nancy may be an embryo author, but Mama and Papa are working at the trade regularly. More than half of their income comes from the love, Western, and sports stories they sell to other editors. Some of their pieces are done on assignment, some on spec. They get rejection slips, but they keep on writing. Irma says she'd still freelance if her editing job paid "ten times as much."

Although most Western pulps concentrate on stories of the old West, *RW* uses stories with a modern flair. "Blood and guts" don't go here. For this magazine, the girl should be aggressive, the complications should come through romantic action, and the climax should be kisses. Most stories are rejected because, as Irma puts it, "They're not for us," or they're in the first person, which is taboo in *RW,* or the writing is just bad. Remembering her own disappointments, Irma tries to reject constructively. Here's a note she wrote to an author who submitted a "not quite":

"You have the makings of a good story in 'Jackpot on Love,' which is

November 1950

enclosed herewith, but somehow, it fails to come off.

"The gambling angle is kind of bad. We don't object to a character gambling—whether he be hero or villain—just as long as the gambling contributes to the progress of the story, or makes for better delineation of character. However, in 'Jackpot on Love,' it doesn't hold water that Steve would gamble away his fortune on a few passes of the dice. You haven't prepared the reader for that sort of person, and so the whole story angle lacks conviction.

"The inheritance angle smacks of being contrived, coming as it does out of a clear blue Western sky. You haven't prepared the reader for it and thus it's too convenient a way to bring in the money. Inheritances, while not exactly a taboo with us, are on our Highly Improbable for Reader Identification List.

"Sherry Travers, of the blond hair, creamy skin and sky-blue Cadillac convertible, never enters the story again after her provocative appearance. And she did start off as though she were going to be a decidedly interesting complication. You certainly whetted our appetite so that we were on the lookout for her again—as a menace. But that was her one and only bid for infamy.

"At the end, too, Lindy's little accident is definitely anti-climactic. After everything is straightened out, all the problems are resolved, and girl has boy, etc.—why toss in the added fillip of having her fall on her head? It's slapstick stuff and detracts from what should have been the ending.

"Sounds like a lot wrong, we know. Perhaps some time you'll care to work it over again."

Harry Steeger seems to have nailed down Irma and Rocky's most admirable accomplishment. Talking about his West Coast editors on a cold, gray day in the East, he said ruefully, "The idea of working in sunny California and drawing a paycheck from New York has a touch of genius about it. They're a couple of smart kids."

[*Author & Journalist*, August 1952]

Wild Editors I Have Known
Thomas Thursday

[What better way to cap off this feast of words than with a slice of devil's food cake from old pal Tom Thursday?]

MOST OF THE FINE EDITORS I STARTED WITH (via Street & Smith and The Frank A. Munsey Company) are dead. And I'd like to interject right here that some of the current crop are half-dead. Nevertheless, on my periodic visits to New York from my home sanctum in Miami, I take them out to dine. I have yet to meet one minus a gourmandizing appetite. But it pays off; and thus we see how literature is oft-times put on a profitable basis. However, before sending an editor a few jars of your homemade preserves, along with your contribution, I might point out that editors print stories, and not preserves. In brief, even the feeding of editors will not yank a check for a bad tale.

Please understand that I am also a learner in the writing vineyards. In writing, no one—and I do mean *no* one—ever learns all about the elusive and mystic art of writing. The fact that I have been in this popular writing racket for so many years does not mean too much. What I am trying to tell you youngsters, and oldsters, is that a writer *never* arrives at the end of learning; even when we reach the end of life we have died without knowing all of writing's manifestations.

I've had perhaps a little more experience battling with the guys and dolls who happen to sit as editors. Such contracts have soured many a new scribe. Time was when I used to bark back at the editorial dogs who had the audacity to toss back my literary-bones with imbecilic criticisms. I soon learned that you can't dam Niagara Falls with the palm of your hand. Moreover, you make enemies; and I had a generous genius for making editorial enemies!

I recall two inane instances wherein I snorted at editorial decisions. For years I had sold tales to a very old he-man magazine, edited by a male who himself was very he-ish. He resigned and his spot was taken by a nice lady. My first contribution to her came back with the suggestion that one of my characters appeared idiotic. I replied, "Since none of the characters are female editors of a man's magazine, madame, I fail to see how they could be idiotic." (Note: My next submission came back with *two* rejection slips).

My second *faux pas* had to do with a very pompous piffle-peddler, this time male, who liked to tear one's yarn apart and insert *his* notions of sound craftsmanship. I took his yammering for three straight stories and then hurled this at his head:

"I have spent the last two days searching for my old Methodist Sunday school teacher. I want to tell her that she took advantage of my youth and lied to me. You know what? She had the nerve to teach me that God was in Heaven. I now know better: he is editing a magazine in New York City."

When you are in this greatest of all crap games for any length of time, why, you soon get the thought that a magazine editor is one who presides over the destinies of a publication to see that nothing interesting gets printed. You may also feel that editors' chief duty is to clip the wings of your ability and imagination and make you safely stupid like themselves. Of course, this is far from true. There are editors and there are idiots.

You must bear in mind that, first, editors are fairly human, like yourself. Some are bright, some are dumb, and some are even sober. Over a long period of years I have met a bushel and I naturally have my favorites. It is easy to select your favorites: they are simply the fellows who buy all you submit to them. Even so, I take none of them too seriously, even when they strut Hitlerian postures. You may have found that the self-inflation of some editors is rather balloonish, albeit the wind is furnished by themselves. Lord knows how many new writers, just ready to spread their wings and fly to fame and fortune, have been clipped in mid-career by stolid, stupid, and sappy editors. I mean, especially, writers who have had a natural gift for a certain type or style of writing, a style that some magazine pilot killed by telling the writer that he or she was on the wrong track.

It has been my considered impression that some editors are sadists. It may be, and perhaps is, due to the fact that they receive such mountains of mucilage that they have become soured and saddened. Day after day, year after year, they receive tons of tripe from infant writers who do not even take the time to learn the fundamentals of construction. But I am not here concerned with the born hopeless hacksmiths. I am concerned with those who have some birth-given talent and have had that talent and ability hounded and hamstrung by certain editors—ladies and gents who were intended by nature to be either stevedores or second-rate beauticians. What, you ask, can be done about such clunkheads in editorial swivels? Well, for one thing, you can have absolute faith in your work, and always recall that writers, like Rome, are not built in a day. If you can really write, you will succeed; don't you *ever* doubt that. Many a writer has thus landed and has had the doubtful pleasure of sticking thumb to nose and making his fingers wave like palm fronds in a hurricane.

Now let us examine, clinically, some editors you are liable to encounter en route to *The Atlantic* and *The Saturday Evening Post*. If your forte is humor, for example, and you are out to succeed Ring Lardner, H.C. Witwer, Damon Runyon, even H. Allen Smith, I herewith extend my hand in anguished sympathy. Although you will have little competition in writing humorous pieces, either fictional or factual, you will have one devil of a time finding editors who can tell a platter of fun from a platter of pastrami. Above all others, beware the editor who tells you that he personally craves humorous stories. Many years ago I was delighted to hear from a lad who confessed that he longed for funny tales in his magazine. I tried him five times and flopped. More, up to the day his magazine went where all bad books go, I never did see a humorous piece in his contents.

As you progress with your tyroship you will meet many weird goblins in the editorial forests. During World War II so many editors were in the services (mostly unarmed, that is) that conditions reached a new low. It seemed that the poor publishers were so hard up for editors that they would rush into the street, stop a bus driver or car-hop girl, and beg, "Say, can you read a little and write a little? You really can? Swell! Come with me—you are going to be my new editor for *True Liars Confessions*."

Judging from some of the letters I have personally received from new editors, I am obliged to assume that there are as many tyro editors as there are tyro writers. Which is a matter of telling you not to take such editors too seriously. They really don't know what it is all about and, if you pay too much attention to their unintelligent bleatings, you are liable to be just as balmy as they are. In efforts to inflate their egos—covering severe inferiority complexes—they may write you advice that will eventually make you a subject for a straitjacket.

Right now, all over this land, there are hundreds, perhaps thousands, of beginning writers who are going nuts trying to fathom what some of these jitney George Horace Lorimers are yapping about. What they are actually trying to do, I sincerely believe, is to impress their publishers. In short, one ass braying for the applause of another. You should know, as I know, that many magazine publishers are not too bright when it comes to plain and even fancy literature. That is why they hire editors. The chief duty of a publisher is to know business and finance. Which, of course, is very important. If he left such matters to the average editor the whole shebang would go to hell. But he naturally expects his editor to know something of script-snapping, and select a story menu that readers can digest without choking from ennui.

But what, exactly, does the average editor know about his readers' likes and dislikes? Most editors live in concrete-based ivory towers and rarely emerge to find out if the magazine is pleasing the readers or not. However, when the publisher calls his attention to the fact that the circulation is going down the chute, the editor gets the notion that he is selecting the wrong wiffle.

I'd like to explode the illusion that editors and writers know what the public wants. In the first place, the public does not know what it wants, until it sees it, and even *then* it can't tell you *why*. No first-rate editor is stupid enough to tell you, or any writer, that he knows what his readers want. Because he does not. All he can do is watch the trends—and there *are* trends—and then hope to God that he can successfully follow them.

Well, then, how far should you go in efforts to please editors? If the fellow is sound and solid and knows his business, I would suggest that you go all the way. *But*—when a tyro author meets a tyro editor, what then? It is quite possible that the tyro writer is a little brighter than the editor. If you are sure—I said *sure*—that your story is the very best you can do, then forget the first editorial criticism and try other editors. If the tale has merit, you will sell it, and you can wager on that.

Every writer worth a pretzel has a certain style, a flair, something that distinguishes him from others. Such writers will encounter some editors who will try to change that style, that born gift, and mold him to their own idiotic conception of what his style should be. It is your duty to forget such editors and continue to be yourself. Imagine, if you can, some editorial dope trying to change the style of H.L. Mencken or George Jean Nathan!

Many of the editors whom I have met in person, at least a hundred over the years, have been more or less prima donnas. They can't conceive of their judgments being wrong. I recall one obdurate gent years ago who told me that I never would sell anything. If he meant real good literary stuff, he was dead right. But if he meant popular padoodle he was 100 percent wrong. And I can show a roomful of published goo to attest the fact. All beginning writers should park the notion that all editors are high and mighty mullahs. I won't hesitate to say that most of them flopped as freelance writers. But they have never given up the thought that, some day, they will make a bum out of Hemingway or Kenneth Roberts. And here's a laugh for you: Two of them actually sent me some of *their* rejected stories, and do you know what? I have a pet talking parrot who can dictate better ones!

I sincerely hope that no one in the audience will take all this as a diatribe against all editors; sour grapes stuff, written by a ham who can't sell a thing he writes. On the contrary, I have made a good living, often very fat, assaulting editors with scores of pop piffle year after year. Right now I have many fine pals in the editorial fields and am not aware of a single enemy.

It is too easy for some editors to get an emperor complex. And when writers agree with their quack judgments, as most of them do, the editor evolves into a dictator. This is bad for both writer and editor. The author is not happy but, since he needs the check, he agrees with anything the dictator says, even though it be the veriest bilge.

I say that such warfare between writers and editors is not too healthy. When a writer disagrees with an editor, and not an ex-hamburger vendor, he will treat your gripes with courtesy and consideration. And it could be that you are *both* mistaken. Moreover, even when the yarn is published a few readers may write in and say the tale is a floperoo.

When it comes to editors, too many authors are yes-men. Of course if you want to sell your soul for a few bucks, that's your affair. But I can tell you this, sir—or ma'am—you can't respect yourself. If you allow editors to punch you in the jaw, without punching back, how can you be anything but a flaming fathead and a spineless sap? Sometimes there is honor among thieves. Can't there be honor among editors and writers?

I wish I could show you the royal road to successful authorship, but have never found the road. I mean to say that, no matter what I write and sell, I find I could have done better after I read the piece in cold type. Meantime, allow me to show you a few words from a greater writer than most of us will ever be—Kenneth L. Roberts. It is taken from the first chapter of *I Wanted To Write*. Here it is:

"I'd like to have it understood in the beginning, and remembered until the end, that these chapters have been written solely because of the staggering number of would-be authors who seem to labor under the delusion that I know a routine, formula, or diet that in a half-hour's time will transform any aspiring young person who admires his own letter-writing ability into a competent and successful novelist. Since there is no such diet, formula, or routine, I have mournfully found it almost impossible to talk to these eager aspirants who want to write—impossible because I also must write, and nobody can produce anything worth printing while talking."

Index

10-Story Detective 124, 129

Abeling, Ruth Agnes 77
Ace-High 15, 16, 34, 44-46, 60
Aces 64
Ace Group 110, 129
Action Stories 16, 39, 99, 101-103, 107, 110
Adventure 18, 27, 33, 40-43, 88, 101, 102, 118
Adventure, March 1934 (cover) 38
Ainslee's 67, 68, 77
Air Adventures 63, 65
Air Force 135
Air Stories 64
All-Fiction 96, 102, 103
All-Story 16, 18, 33, 36, 67, 73, 79, 117
All Detective 110, 111
All in the Family 154
All Quiet on the Western Front 110
All Sports 148
All Western 110
Amazing Stories 121, 130, 136
American, The 51, 131
American Expeditionary Force 70, 91
American Fiction Guild 70, 93, 130
American Mercury, The 51, 83
American Parade, The 68
American Weekly 133, 136
Anderson, Sherwood 9
Andersonville 79
Argosy 16, 18, 27, 33, 36-38, 67, 87, 88, 104, 117, 118, 132
Arie, Mark 71
Arnold, Major H.H. 72
Astounding 70, 130
As Dead As It Gets 154
Atlantic, The 51, 159
Austin, Diane 154
Authors' League Bulletin, The 55
Author & Journalist, The 41, 70

Bacon, Daisy 2, 77, 127, 128
Bacon, Daisy (photo) 78
Baird, Edwin 79
Baird, Edwin (photo) 79
Ball, William David 63
Balmer, Edwin 132
Bamber, Wallace R. 7, 92, 102
Bamber, Wallace R. (photo) 93
Bartlett, John T. 70
Bartlett, Margaret 70
Bates, Harry 130
Batman 133
Battle Stories 69, 71, 99, 103
Bean, "Bunker" 81
Beaver, The 133
Bedford-Jones, H. 87, 92, 95, 102
Beim, Gerrold 136
Best Detective 57
Bittner, A.H. 16, 27, 28, 31, 33, 87, 99
Blackwell, Frank E. 2, 16, 21, 22, 24-26, 57
Black Mask 132
Bloberger, Chief 71
Blood 'n' Thunder 87
Blue Book 104
Blue Ribbon Magazines 139
Bookman, The 83
Book of the Dead 89
Bosworth, Allan 111, 125
Boy's Work 33
Bradfield, Harriet A. 85
Breezy Point Lodge 71
Breezy Stories 67
Brief Stories 67, 68
Bromfield, Louis 78
Bromley, Snowshoe Al 81
Brooklyn Eagle, The 67, 68
Bruce, George 130, 132
Brundage, Margaret 2
Burks, Arthur J. 63, 79, 110, 130
Burks, Arthur J. (photo) 66
Burn, Witch, Burn 133
Burnham, Major Frederick R. 74

Burns, Walter Noble 74
Butler, Ellis Parker 9
Butterick Publishing Company 27, 41
Byrne, Jack 102, 132

Camp-Fire, The 33, 42
Captain Billy's Whiz Bang 69-71
Captain Marvel 69
Carter, Bob 64
Cavalcade of America 118, 134
Cavalier, The 33, 70, 73
CBS 69
Century, The 51, 83
Cerf, Bennett 73
Chesterfield Publications 139
Chicago Herald-Examiner 90
Chicago Tribune 90
Churchill, Edward 133
City of Purple Dreams, The 81
Clancy, Eugene A. 27, 110
Clayton, W.M. 44
Clayton Publications 34, 61, 63, 65
Clemenceau, Georges 68
Clues 15, 27, 44, 60, 80
Colgate Comedy Hour, The 154
College Humor 79, 80
Collegiate World Publishing Company 80
Collier, Edmund 73
Collier's 13, 18, 80, 132
Colt, Thatcher 132
Columbia Publications 139
Comet, The 121
Complete Aviation Novel Magazine 92
Complete Stories 104
Comstock, Henry B. 118
Conflict 92
Coronet 134-137
Cosmopolitan 18, 27, 132
Country Gentleman 132
Country Life Press 28, 73
Cowboy Stories 16, 34, 44, 46, 60
Cox, Mr. 42

Crawford, Broderick 134
Crawford, William H. 139
Crest Books 69
Crime Mysteries 21
Cupid's Diary 85, 86, 101
Curry, Tom 79

Daigh, Ralph 69, 101
Daily News 81
Dance Magazine, The 68
Danger Trail, The 44
Davis, Elmer 78
Davis, Robert H. 10-12, 14, 16, 34-36, 48
Delineator, The 41
Dell Publishing 21, 87, 99, 110
Dent, Lester 99, 130
Denver Times, The 73
Detective-Dragnet 96
Detective Fiction Weekly 27, 80
Detective Story 15, 16, 18, 21, 27, 57, 58, 77, 127
Detective Tales 79, 90
de Grouchy, William 77
Doc Savage 77, 92
Dold, Elliott 2
Donnel, C.P. Jr. 125
Double-Action Group 139
Doubleday, Doran & Company 27, 73, 87
Doubleday, Page & Company 16, 27, 28, 31, 73, 75
Dragnet, The 60
Dreiser, Theodore 77, 125
Dublin, Frances 67
Dunn, J. Allan 87, 92

Eagles of the Air 92
Eastern Distributing Corporation, The 60
Echols, Allan K. 63-65
Edwards, John F. 60
Eliot, George Fielding 133
Elite Styles Magazine 60
Ellsworth, Fanny 132
Ellsworth, Whitney 133, 135
Elmer Gantry 71

Ernst, Paul 130, 132
Esquire 79
Everybody's 27, 33, 41, 43, 67
Excitement 83, 104

Famous First Facts 136
Famous Lives 85
Famous Western 148
Fantascience Digest 139
Fantastic Adventures 121
Far East Adventure Stories 92-94, 96, 97, 102
Far West 15, 21, 57, 58
Fate 121
Fawcett, Captain Roscoe 2, 69
Fawcett, Captain W.H. 70
Fawcett, Captain W.H. (photo) 69
Fawcett, Gordon W. 69
Fawcett, Roger K. 69
Fawcett, Roscoe K. 69
Fawcett, W.H. Jr. 69
Fawcett Publications 69, 71
Fay, Bill 132
Feininger, Andreas 134
Feldman, Anatole 92
Fiction House 16, 34, 39, 40, 63, 64, 73, 85, 99, 102, 110
Field, Dick 137
Fisher, Steve 130, 131
Five-Novels 104
Fletcher, J.S. 102
Flyers 63
Flying Aces 60
flying saucers 121
Ford, T.W. 148
Forester, Eddie 125
Fowler, Dan 133
Frank A. Munsey Company, The 10, 33, 34, 117, 118, 158
Free Lance Weekly, The 57
Friend, Oscar J. 124, 126, 133
Frontier, The 16, 18, 27, 28, 31, 75, 88
Frontier Stories 73
Future Fiction 139
F Troop 154

G-8 and His Battle Aces 85
Gable, Clark 131
Gangland Stories 96
Gangster Stories 96
Gang World 96
Gardner, Erle Stanley 125
George H. Doran Company 27
Gernsback, Hugo 121, 130
Ghost Stories 67
Gibson, Walter 57
Ginsberg, Irma 154
Golden Argosy, The 33
Golden West, The 60
Goldsmith, Harold 110
Gold Medal Books 69
Golenpaul, Dan 136
Good Times 154
Graeve, Oscar 43
Graves, Peggy 154
Greene, Lewis 134
Green Valley, USA 134
Gruber, Frank 79, 130, 132
Guenther, John 133
Gunsmoke 154
Gun Molls 96
Gurian, Naomi 154

Halston, Don 136
Hammett, Dashiell 27
Hammond, Harold 139
Hardy, Bob 108
Harper's 51, 83
Harper & Brothers 67, 68
Harte, Bret 68
Haunting Hand, The 67
Hawkins, Willard E. 14, 34, 69, 98
Haycox, Ernest 73
Hayes, William Edward 117, 118
Health 90
Hearst's International 13, 51, 67
Hemingway, Ernest 161
Hendryx, James B. 74

Henneberger, J.C. 79
Henry, O. 84
Hersey, Harold 16, 41, 44, 47, 60, 70, 85, 110
Hersey, Harold (portrait) 62
Heywood, Bill 75
High Spot Magazine 104
Hoffman, Arthur Sullivant 42, 88
Holden, William 134
Horn, Roy de S. 73, 101, 104
Hornig, Charles D. 121
Hotaling, Charles 137
Hubbard, Freeman H. 2, 7, 117, 118
Humphrey, Joa 77
Hutchings, Ed Jr. 137
Hygiea 81

Illustrated World 27
Information, Please 136
I Wanted To Write 162

Jack and Jill 118
James, Will 74
Jemail, Jimmy 137
Jenkins, George Briggs 41
Johnson, W. Ryerson 124, 128, 129, 133
Jones, Beatrice 133
Jones, Robert Gibson 2

Kalian, Cady 154
Kalish, Austin "Rocky" 154-157
Kalish, Irma 7, 154-157
Kaltenborn, H.V. 67
Kane, Joseph Nathan 136
Kantor, MacKinley 79
Keeler, Harry Stephen 81
Kelly, "Commando" 135
Kelly, J.B. 16, 39, 63, 64, 85, 102
Kessler, Hazlett 27
Kipling, Rudyard 84, 96, 113, 114
Kirby, Dan 148

Lagerlof, Selma 74

Lampell, Millard 133
Lardner, Ring 159
Lariat, The 16, 39, 99
Lariat Story 100, 101, 110
Laurel, The 90
Laurence, John I. 104
Lear, Norman 154
Ledernier Cri, The 60
Lee, B. Virginia 85, 87
Lee, Dick 136
Lee, Lawrence 7, 83
Lengel, William C. 13, 14
Lenniger, August 79, 125, 128
Lewis, Jerry 154
Lewis, Sinclair 71
Liberty 79, 118, 132, 137
Lichtblau, Joseph 85
Life 134
Life on the Mississippi 128
Lindbergh, Charles 95, 97
Little Knight of the X Bar B 74
Little Women 77
London Daily Mail 133
Long, Ray 27, 67
Lorimer, George Horace 160
Lovecraft, H.P. 79
Lovers Magazine 85
Love and War Stories 110
Love Romances 39, 85, 86
Love Story 77, 78, 101
Love Story Writer 77
Lowndes, Robert A.W. 8, 121, 139
Lowndes, Robert A.W. (photo) 140

Macfadden Publications 60
MacLean, Charles Agnew 83
Madison Eagle 88
Magazine Digest 136
Magazine Publishers 60, 110
Magic Carpet Magazine, The 89
Mammoth Detective 124, 136
Man Stories 96

Margulies, Leo 126, 127, 131, 135, 138
Martin, Dean 154
Martin, Peter 135
Martin, Tony 134
Martinsen, Richard A. 7, 16, 33, 39, 40, 99, 110
Martinsen, Richard A. (photo) 99
Martin and Lewis Show, The 154
Maule, Harry E. 14, 16, 27, 28, 31, 32, 73, 87, 88
Maule, Harry E. (photo) 74
Maule, John Penrose 74
Maule, Mary K. 73, 74
McClure, S.S. 83
McFee, William 74
McIlwraith, Dorothy 73
McKinnon-Fly Company 67
Meet Corliss Archer 154
Mencken, H.L. 112, 161
Merritt, A. 133
Merriwell, Frank 41, 57
Metronome 133
Mexican Daily Record, The 73
Millay, Edna St. Vincent 67
Miller, Glenn 134
Minneapolis Tribune 69
Mix, Tom 71
Modern Love 101
Modern Mechanics 71
Movie Monthly 68
Mowre, Carson 2, 99, 103, 110
Mulford, Clarence E. 74
Mundy, Talbot 87
Munsey, Frank A. 33, 37
Munsey's 16, 33, 35, 67, 90
Murray, Will 87
Musical America 83
Mystery Magazine 16, 33, 38
My Favorite Martian 154
My Three Sons 154

Nathan, George Jean 161
Nation, The 83
National Sunday Magazine 68

Navy Blue and Gold 132
Navy Stories 99
Newsweek 133
New Love 154
New Pulpwood Editor, The 41
New York Globe 88
New York Herald 57
New York Market Letter 85
New York Press 73
New York Sun 57, 73
New York Times 69, 77
Northwest Stories 16, 39, 99
Not Too Narrow, Not Too Deep 131

"off-trail" 152
Oregonian, The 69
Oriental Stories 89, 90, 96, 97
Oursler, Fulton 132
Outlaws of the West 70
Overland Monthly, The 68

Packard, Frank L. 87
Painton, Frederick C. 130, 131
Palmer, Loren 13
Palmer, Ray 2, 7, 121, 136
Palmer, Ray (photo) 122
Palmer Institute of Authorship, The 63
Palmer Photoplay Corporation, The 63
paper shortage 124
Parade 135
Park, Marie Antoinette 139
Parker, Dorothy 127
Peanuts 69
Pearson's 67
Pen and Pencil Club 129
People's Home Journal, The 83
Perkins, Lynn 135
Perry, Ralph 16
Pershing, John Joseph 71
Pete Rice 92
Pictorial Review 18, 51
Pierce, Frank Richardson 130, 132

Pines, Ned 69
Plain Tales From the Hills 114
Popular Detective 124
Popular Fiction Institute 27
Popular Fiction Publishing Company 90
Popular Library 69
Popular Magazine, The 104
Popular Mechanics 118
Popular Photography 135
Popular Publications 85, 110, 118, 124, 154, 155
Popular Science 118
Price, E. Hoffmann 89
Prison Stories 96
Proctor, A.A. 102
Proust, Marcel 152
Prudential Hour, The 134
"pulp," use of 28
pulprack.com 28
Pulp Fictioneers 92, 111
Pulp Jungle, The 79

Quick Trigger Western 85
Quill, The 60
Quinn, Seabury 79

Racketeer Stories 96
Radio City Playhouse 57
Railroad 118
Railroad Avenue, Great Stories and Legends of American Railroading 118
Railroad Camera Club 117
Railroad Magazine 118
Railroad Man's Magazine 117-120
Railroad Stories 118
Raine, William MacLeod 73
Ranch Romances 44
Random House 73
Rangeland Romances 154
Rascoe, Burton 27
Reader's Digest 132, 137
Real America 79
Real Detective Tales 79-81
Real Love Magazine 77

Redbook 132
Red Book 18, 27, 51
Reusswig, William 2
Richards, Edmund C. 104
Riders of the Range 85
Rittenhouse, Jessie B. 83
RKO Pictures 73
Roberts, Kenneth 161, 162
Roberts, W. Adolphe 2, 7, 67, 68
Roberts, W. Adolphe (photo) 68
Roberts, Walter Adolf 67
Rogers, Joel Townsley 105
Rogers, Wayne 87
Romance (1928-29) 27
Romance (1937-54) 154
Romance Western 154, 155
Romance Western Roundup 154
Romantic Range 77
Roscoe, Theodore 92
Rosmond, Babette 77
Rozen, George 2
Ruber, Peter 27
Rud, Anthony 16, 27, 31
Rud, Anthony (photo) 32
Runyon, Damon 159
Russell, Charles 2
Russell, Charles M. 74

Saint Detective Magazine, The 79
Sale, Chic 104
Sale, Richard 130, 131
Salz, H. Wolff 124
Sanger, Margaret 67
San Francisco Chronicle 68
Saturday Evening Post, The 18, 27, 48, 51, 77, 78, 80, 107, 118, 131, 159
Saturday Review 83
Science Fiction 139
Scienti-Snaps 139
Scotland Yard 99
Scott, Arthur E. 12, 13, 31, 41, 43, 48, 49, 54
Scott, Arthur E. (photo) 54
Scott, Sir Walter 89

Screen Secrets 71
Scribner's 51, 83
Seabrook, William 136
Sea Stories 83, 84
Secret Agent X 130
Seltzer, Charles Alden 74
Sessions, A.L. 83
Seven Footprints to Satan 133
Shadow, The 57, 77
Shaver, Richard 121
Shaver Mystery 121
Shaw, George Bernard 143
Shevelson, Harris 134
Short Stories 14-16, 18, 27, 31, 73, 75, 88, 102, 104
Silberkleit, Louis H. 139
Simon, Dick 133
Simon, George 133
Simpson, Robert 16, 33, 37
Skyways 135
Sky Riders 99
Sloane, T. O'Conor 121
Smart Love Stories 77
Smart Set, The 67
Smiley, Dr. William H. 74
Smith, Clark Ashton 79
Smith, H. Allen 159
Smith's Magazine 77
Spanish-American War 70
Spider, The 85
Sport Story 83, 84
St. Clair, Margaret 121
Standard Magazines 125
"Standish, Burt L." 41
Starrett, Vincent 79, 81
Star Magazine 96
Star Western 85
Steeger, Harry 99, 110, 154, 155, 157
Steger, Harry Peyton 73
Stein, Modest 2
Stewart, James 132
Stewart, Jeanne 85
Stone, Albert William 15, 41

Strange Cargo 131
Street & Smith 12, 21, 23, 24, 27, 31, 34, 41, 43, 44, 57, 77, 78, 127, 131, 158
Stribling, T.S. 74
Strope, Alice 16, 21, 22, 25
Student Writer, The (column) 70
Student Writer, The (magazine) 41, 57, 70
Summer Goes On 83
Sun, The 35, 36
Superman 133, 135
Swap 60
Sweetheart Stories 101
Syracuse University 154

Taylor, Merlin 81
Teck Publications 121
Telling Tales 44
Ten Detective Aces 129
Terrill, Rogers 127, 132
Third Book of Modern Verse 83
This Week 132, 135, 137
Thomas, Henry Wilton 9, 10, 12, 41
Thrilling Adventures 92
Thrilling Detective 92
Thrilling Wonder Stories 70
Thursday, Thomas 9, 158
Time Traveler, The 130
Tinsley, Ted 130, 132
Titherington, Richard H. 16, 35
Tolstoy, Leo 152
Top-Notch 9, 12, 31, 41, 43, 44, 48, 104
Toronto Star Weekly 136
Tower Publications 107
Triple-X 69, 71, 99
Triple-X Western 69, 101
Troeh, Frank 71
True 118
True Adventures 99
True Confessions 71
True Love Affairs 72
True Story Magazine 86
True Western Stories 16

Tully, Jim 114
Twain, Mark 114, 128

Underworld, The 60
Underworld Magazine, The 96
Under Fire Magazine 60, 92
United Press, The 73, 75
Universal Newsreels 136
University of Virginia Magazine 83
Unusual Stories 139

Virginian, The 74
Virginia Quarterly Review 83

War Aces 99, 110
War Birds 92, 110
War Novels 99, 110
War Romances 110
War Stories 87, 92, 99, 103, 110
Waters, Alan 133
Watson, Emmett 2
Weaver, Walter R. 135
Webb, Jean Francis 130
Weird Tales 27, 70, 79, 89, 90
Weisinger, Mort 130
Weisinger, Mort (photo) 130
West 16, 27, 31, 73, 75, 100, 101
Western Federation 75
Western Rangers 70
Western Romances 87, 110
Western Story 16, 18, 21, 22, 57, 58, 101, 102
Western Trails 15, 60, 70
White, Matthew Jr. 16, 33, 35, 49
White, Matthew Jr. (photo) 36
White, Rusty 108
Whiting, John 135
Widmer, Harry 154
Williams, Ben Ames 114
Winchell, Walter 132
Winford Publications 139
Wings 64, 110
Winn, Mary Day 132

Winnipeg Free Press 69
Witwer, H.C. 9, 159
Wolf, Kenneth 136
Wollheim, Donald 129
Wonder Stories 121, 130
wood-pulp magazines 51
Woodford, Jack 81
Woolworth's 107
World War II; editors in the service 160
Wright, Farnsworth 2, 89, 97
Writer's Digest, November 1950 (cover) 156
Writer's Digest 85, 92, 111, 121, 144, 154
Writer's Review 99
Writers' Markets and Methods 63, 87
Writers Guild of America 154
Wylie, Philip 132
Wyn, A.A. 27, 99, 110

Ziff-Davis Publishing 121
Zubryn, Emil 57

ALSO FROM OFF-TRAIL PUBLICATIONS:

The Weird Detective Adventures of Wade Hammond
by Paul Chadwick
10 stories from *Detective-Dragnet* and *Ten Detective Aces*
180 pages, $18

The City of Baal
by Charles Beadle
7 stories of African adventure
from *Adventure* and *The Frontier*
240 pages, $20

Check or MO to:
Off-Trail Publications
2036 Elkhorn Road
Castroville, CA 95012
Paypal: offtrail@redshift.com

www.ingramcontent.com/pod-product-compliance
Lightning Source LLC
Chambersburg PA
CBHW032118090426
42743CB00007B/389